Steve Legg is a unique and creative communicator. He is committed to educating the unchurched about the relevance of Christianity in as many different ways as possible. If you want to pick up a lot of good ideas, then this is the book to get them from.

J John

Steve Legg doesn't just wax eloquently about evangelism – he lives it. He also personifies the glorious madness and passion of a true evangelist – which I believe you will catch through the words of this book. Creative, disturbing, empowering stuff – I commend the man and his words without hesitation.

Jeff Lucas

I'm not sure I like Christians very much, but I like Steve Legg. He is a rare kind of Christian. Buy [the book], read it and follow Steve's example. At the very least, you could have a whole lot more fun.

Eric Delve

Steve is a man who does not just preach to the lost, he actually takes time to love and befriend them. He believes in showing them about Jesus, not just telling them about him. That makes this book a genuine read from a genuine evangelist.

Ishmael

I thank God for your liberating message.

Rt Hon. and Most Rev. George Carey,
Lord Archbishop of Canterbury

Every time I look at his books I roar with laughter.

Paul Archer — Steve's accountant

I've been a neighbour of Steve's for over three years and during that time we have become great friends. As a non-Christian myself, Steve always respects my views and doesn't try to force religion on me. In his laid-back approach to religion he does get his message across, but always finds time for a chat, a joke and a pint.

Scott Jones — Steve's neighbour

The A–Z
of Evangelism

The Ultimate Guide
to Sharing Your Faith

Steve Legg

Hodder & Stoughton
LONDON SYDNEY AUCKLAND

Copyright © 2002 by Steve Legg

First published in Great Britain in 2002

The right of Steve Legg to be identified as the Author of
the Work has been asserted by him in accordance
with the Copyright, Designs and Patents Act 1988.

10 9 8 7 6 5 4 3 2 1

British Library Cataloguing in Publication Data
A record for this book is available from the British Library

ISBN 0 340 78638 8

Typeset by Avon Dataset Ltd, Bidford-on-Avon, Warks

Printed and bound in Great Britain by
Clays Ltd, St Ives plc

Hodder & Stoughton
A Division of Hodder Headline Ltd
338 Euston Road
London NW1 3BH

Through thick and thin, keep your hearts at attention, in adoration before Christ, your Master. Be ready to speak up and tell anyone who asks why you're living the way you are.

Peter the Apostle
Martyred in Rome, AD 65
(1 Peter 3:14–15, *The Message*)

Contents

Acknowledgements

This book was written in the 2000/2001 football season during which Micky Adams skilfully steered our beloved Brighton and Hove Albion into the Second Division, becoming Division Three Champions and winning their first title in thirty-six years in the process. Thank you for your inspiration, Micky, and for bringing hope back to Seagulls fans everywhere.

On the subject of inspiration, this book would probably never have happened if it hadn't been for great friends who have helped and inspired me with their words, actions and friendship over the years. So a huge thank you to Ishmael, J. John, Jeff Lucas, Eric Delve, Paul Bennison and Nick Mitchell. Also thanks to Jill Troup at *Idea* magazine who so kindly allowed me to use a great big chunk of an article about the Internet that she wrote so much better than I could ever have done.

I'm eternally grateful to my trustees – Paul Archer, Andy Economides and Jonathan McClelland – whose advice and friendship have guided and steered the ministry so well, and to our faithful prayer partners who through their prayer and practical help have kept us going. I wouldn't be able to do what I'm doing without you. Also thank you to David Moloney and his fantastic team at Hodder and Stoughton for believing in me and sharing my excitement about this book.

Finally, thank you to my wonderful children – Jay, Amber, Emmie and Maddie – who have understood when Daddy was too busy to play football or go over to the park because he was busy writing, and lastly, to my gorgeous wife, Jemma, who is my harshest critic, yet one of the kindest people I know, and has taught me so much about putting others first. Darling, you mean more to me than I can ever say.

About the Author

Steve Legg is an evangelist, escapologist, author and Director of the Breakout Trust, a UK-based charity committed to communicating the relevance of the Christian faith. This is done through a variety of ways including trickery, mystery, comedy and escapology. Dangerous and daring escapes suspended from cranes or manacled between high-powered jeeps going in opposite directions have brought massive attention to Steve's abilities to draw and entertain large crowds across the world.

As well as entertaining, Steve often uses his skills to communicate a powerful message of freedom through Christianity. Steve talks and demonstrates his talents in schools, colleges, universities, pubs, night clubs and out onto the streets, from Portland Prison to Canterbury Cathedral – in fact wherever people are.

Steve travels the length and breadth of the United Kingdom as well as working in various countries across the world. He has been privileged to work with a whole list of household names including Jonathan Ross, Gloria Hunniford, Fern Britton, Paul Ross, Helen Shapiro, Gloria Gaynor, Boyzone, Roger Whittaker, Zoe Ball, Keith Chegwin, Phillipa Forrester, top Radio 1 DJ Mark Radcliffe, Don Maclean, Lorraine Chase, Josie D'Arby and Brit-pop band, Republica, to name just a few!

He has appeared on national television on numerous occasions, and his impressive list of TV credits include *How 2*, *The Big Breakfast* and *The Disney Club* right through to *Songs of Praise*. In 1995, Steve was part of the *Cannon and Ball Gospel Show* that toured the UK. This major tour covered a staggering forty-eight dates across the nation, making it one of the biggest gospel tours ever produced. The show was also the subject for a BBC special documentary, and became the number one best-selling video of its kind.

On top of all this, Steve is also an accomplished presenter, broadcaster and writer. He has written a number of small booklets for CPO, the Christian literature charity based in Worthing. His first paperback, *Making Friends – Evangelism the Easy Way* was written for Christians, equipping them to share their faith more effectively. Then *Man, Myth or Maybe More?* was released in March 1999; this examined the life of Jesus, from his birth in a smelly shed, through a life full of incredible occurrences, to his death at the hands of his fellow countrymen and onto the greatest comeback of all time. Later that year, *Big Questions* followed where Steve attempted in his laid-back way to answer over thirty tough questions that are asked about God, Jesus, life and the universe.

He is married to Jemma, and has four small children – Jay, Amber, Emmie and Maddie – and they are all part of Arun Community Church in Littlehampton, West Sussex. Steve is also a member of the Rustington Sports and Social Club, Equity, London's prestigious Magic Circle and is a very proud member of the Curry Club.

Foreword

Books on the subject of personal evangelism appear in the Christian Church at regular intervals. They also seem to disappear just as quickly. In my experience most of these books seem to work on guilt in order to motivate the people of God to evangelise and then proceed to give a few hints or techniques as to how this difficult task can be carried out by ordinary people, most of whom feel completely ill-equipped to do so.

The efforts of these authors may be worthy and they may motivate some of us to a kind of ill-at-ease attempt to 'evangelise our neighbours, friends and relations'. In due time, many of them learn to see us coming and avoid us like the plague.

I'm not sure I like Christians very much, but I like Steve Legg. He is a rare kind of Christian, a real human being who lets the presence of Jesus bubble out of him quite naturally. If more of us were like him, more people in the world would see Jesus and follow him.

Come to think of it, that's just what this book is all about. Buy it, read it and follow Steve's example. At the very least, you could have a whole lot more fun.

Eric Delve, evangelist

Introduction

Conrad Hilton was born in San Antonio, USA, and began his career by renting out rooms in his home. He took a job as a local bank cashier and was so successful that he soon purchased a bank of his own. He assumed control of a small hotel in Texas in 1919 and over the next sixty years built up an international hospitality empire. Just before he died, Hilton was asked if he had any last words of wisdom for the world. This is what he said: *'Leave the shower curtain on the inside of the tub.'*

Marie Antoinette was the wife of King Louis XVI of France. In 1793 she was convicted of treason following the Revolution and sentenced to death by beheading. As she approached the guillotine, she accidentally stepped on the foot of her executioner. Consequently, her last words recorded for posterity were: *'Pardonnez-moi, Monsieur.'*

Lady Nancy Astor was the first woman Member of Parliament. Noted for her biting wit, she occasionally got into verbal spats with Winston Churchill. She spoke her last words when, on her deathbed, she momentarily awoke to find herself surrounded by her entire family and asked those present: *'Am I dying or is this my birthday?'*

Unlike the German economist, philosopher and revolutionary, Karl Marx, who considered: *'Last words are for fools who haven't said enough'*, Jesus had plenty to say and consequently chose his last words very carefully. He'd lived for thirty-three years as a man, had been murdered and then came back to life. Just before

1

he left his disciples to ascend to heaven, he spoke to them one last time:

> All authority in heaven and on earth has been given to me. Therefore go and make disciples of all nations, baptising them in the name of the Father and of the Son and of the Holy Spirit, and teaching them to obey everything I have commanded you. And surely I am with you always, to the very end of the age. (Matthew 28:18–20)

Jesus left his followers with that important task – the Great Commission. The early Church got on with the task with great success and enthusiasm. Some 2,000 years later, the job is still unfinished. According to the US Census Office, the world's population on 31 December 2000 was 6,118,958,932. Of that 6.12 billion, around 11 per cent of the world's population claim to know Jesus as their personal Saviour. The rate of increase is around 7 per cent annually, compared to 2.6 per cent for Islam. Patrick Johnson estimates that between 75 and 85 per cent of people in the world have heard of Jesus. Wonderful, isn't it? But that still means at least 15 per cent of the world have still to hear. God has left the job in our hands. The thing is though, many of us find evangelism difficult, and that's why I felt I should write this book.

The satellite music channel, MTV, surveyed 1,600 teenagers from different European countries in 1996. Of the young Britons interviewed, 48 per cent believed in God, 4 per cent went to church, 15 per cent visited mediums, 22 per cent indulged in tarot cards or palm reading and 21 per cent had used a ouija board at some time.

In a Gallup poll, reported in the *Daily Telegraph* (16 December 1999), less than half the population of Britain believes in Jesus, with 14 per cent claiming not to know who he is. The number of people who believe that Jesus is the Son of God has fallen from 71 per cent in 1957 to 45 per cent in 1999. Another 22 per cent believe he is 'just a story'. In a more recent MORI poll (14 January 2000) where interviewees were asked whom they found inspirational, Nelson Mandela, Richard Branson, Margaret

Thatcher and even Britney Spears scored higher than Jesus, who received just 1 per cent of the votes cast. These figures could be seen as depressing, but I see them as a challenge to more effective evangelism.

I don't profess to be an expert on the subject – though since 1988 I have done evangelism as my main job, so I'd have to be pretty daft not to have learned a thing or two. The contents in this book aren't all original to me either. I'm sure probably most of the better ideas here have been pinched from someone else, so if you're reading this and recognise something you might have said or written about, then do forgive me, though I take some comfort in the words of Mark Twain who suggested that Adam was the only person who ever had anything completely original to say!

The word *evangel,* from 'evangelism', literally means 'good news' – it's a message – though these messages are too often conveyed in words. We seem to forget, all too easily, that actually evangelism and witnessing are more than just words. I do believe most of us have forgotten how to be good news. Instead of actually doing it we just talk and preach about it.

Deep down we do believe in evangelism, and a lot of books are written and conferences held to discuss it, though for many it remains just a theoretical thing. Let's learn afresh how to share the glorious good news of the gospel, but most of all let's learn how to be good news.

Steve Legg
May 2001

Ananias

Evangelism. Perhaps a word that fills you with terror because you know you should be doing it, but feel that you can't. Maybe you feel you don't read your Bible enough, or pray enough, or know enough about theology to properly explain the gospel. It could be that you've already made your mind up – evangelism is for the experts.

I have to say that this is not the case. If we're honest, none of us pray or read our Bibles enough and we all make mistakes from time to time. None of us are good enough. The good news is this: God loves to use ordinary people like you and me who feel they don't qualify. General Eisenhower once rebuked one of his generals for referring to a soldier as 'just a private'. He reminded him that the army could function better without its generals than it could without its foot-soldiers. '*If this war is to be won*,' he said, '*it will be won by privates*.' In the same way if the gospel is to be taken to the lost, it is us *ordinary* Christians who should be doing it.

Jesus' twelve disciples were a motley crew of ordinary men from varied backgrounds with different occupations and person-alities. James, John, Simon and Andrew were fishermen. They probably owned their own boats and had flourishing businesses, yet they left all of that to follow Jesus. Matthew was a very wealthy tax collector and Simon the Zealot belonged to a nationalist group whose aim was to overthrow the Romans and free Israel. Judas Iscariot was the group's treasurer and Philip was the neighbour of Simon Peter and Andrew. He in turn told

Bartholomew that he had found the Messiah. Thomas has been nicknamed 'Doubting Thomas' who ceased to doubt after he had met the risen Jesus. Indeed, legend tells us that Thomas was killed by a lance at Coromandel in the East Indies, rather than refute his faith. We don't know much about James and Judas, apart from the fact that they and the others were ordinary people that Jesus chose to alter the course of history.

You and I are probably quite ordinary too, but Jesus sees tremendous potential in us and wants to use us to reach others for him. I want to start this book on evangelism with the wonderful story of a man named Ananias who once again was very ordinary, but was used by God in an incredible way. Here's the story about his encounter with a nasty piece of work called Saul:

In Damascus there was a disciple named Ananias. The Lord called to him in a vision, 'Ananias!'

'Yes, Lord,' he answered.

The Lord told him, 'Go to the house of Judas on Straight Street and ask for a man from Tarsus named Saul, for he is praying. In a vision he has seen a man named Ananias come and place his hands on him to restore his sight.'

'Lord,' Ananias answered, 'I have heard many reports about this man and all the harm he has done to your saints in Jerusalem. And he has come here with authority from the chief priests to arrest all who call on your name.'

But the Lord said to Ananias, 'Go! This man is my chosen instrument to carry my name before the Gentiles and their kings and before the people of Israel. I will show him how much he must suffer for my name.'

Then Ananias went to the house and entered it. Placing his hands on Saul, he said, 'Brother Saul, the Lord – Jesus, who appeared to you on the road as you were coming here – has sent me so that you may see again and be filled with the Holy Spirit.' Immediately, something like scales fell from Saul's eyes, and he could see again. He got up and was baptised, and after taking some food, he regained his strength.

Saul spent several days with the disciples in Damascus. At once he began to preach in the synagogues that Jesus is the Son of God. (Acts 9:10–20)

As you probably know, Saul – who of course became the great apostle, Paul – started off as an enemy of Christians. He had been persecuting them in Jerusalem and was now on his way to Damascus to extradite others. His journey would have been made on foot and probably took about a week. Saul's only companions were the officers of the Sanhedrin, a kind of police force. Because Saul was a Pharisee, he wouldn't have anything to do with these other men, so he walked by himself, and probably thought a great deal – after all, there was nothing else to do. As he finished his 140-mile journey and was finally on the outskirts of Damascus, a bright light from heaven suddenly flashed around him, and he heard the voice of Jesus. Saul immediately surrendered his life to Jesus and entered the city a changed man. He was told to wait for a man named Ananias.

What a powerful story! We're going to look a little closer at what happened – in particular at how significant Ananias's role was, in probably the most famous conversion story in history – and see what we can learn from it.

Be ready

When God spoke to Ananias his response was: '*Yes, Lord*' (v. 10). Quite simply, Ananias was ready to be used by God. He was told he must go and see Saul; he was even directed to the right house. God is desperate to use us, so let's be ready to seize any opportunity. I'll be sharing later in this book how God once used me in incredible ways at an occult festival on the other side of the world. Hundreds became Christians – not because of anything special that I did, but because I was ready and available to God.

Consider this modern parable. A man came up to a taxi-driver in New York and said, 'Take me to London.' The taxi-driver told him there was no possible way for him to drive the cab across the Atlantic. The customer insisted there was.

'You'll drive me down to the pier and we'll put the taxi on a freighter and when we get off at Liverpool, you'll drive me to London and I'll pay you whatever is on the meter.' The driver agreed and when they arrived in London, good to his word, the passenger paid the total on the meter and gave a hundred-pound tip. The cab-driver roamed around London and didn't know what to do.

Another man hailed him and said 'I want you to drive me to New York.' The cab-driver couldn't believe his good luck. I mean, how often can you pick up a fare in London who wants to go to New York? The passenger says, 'First, we take a boat . . .'

The driver said, 'That I know. But where to in New York?'

The passenger said, 'Riverside Drive and 104th Street.'

And the driver responded, 'Sorry, I don't go to the west side.'

Be ready and prepared for any job, however unlikely it might sound.

Be available

Ananias must have thought he was going stark staring mad when God told him the name of the man he was to go and meet. Saul was known as a murderer of Christians. Indeed there probably wasn't a man living or dead whom Ananias was more afraid of, and here was God telling him to go and speak to him. God had even told him why he must go, and two reasons were given: first, that Saul was already praying and was now ready; and second, that he had been shown a vision of a man named Ananias coming to pray for him.

God was arranging what I like to call a 'divine appointment'. Divine appointments work and they work well. I could tell you of hundreds of occasions when I have connected with people in the most extraordinary ways and I'm sure you can think of your own examples. Let me share one with you. I was with a small team working in Paris, helping a Tamil church with evangelism in the city. It was our night off, so I and my friend Andy, who was working with a church in Tooting, London for a year, decided to go up the Eiffel Tower. We had a good look around, and I prayed that God would give us one of these divine appointments with someone.

Coming back down in the crowded lift, I felt a real compulsion to preach the gospel. I figured that I'd have a captive audience for at least two minutes, so I gave it a go. As I launched into my explanation of the gospel, some people seemed interested and some looked very embarrassed, but when we got out we struck up a conversation with a guy from New Zealand who was on holiday. He'd been very impressed with what I'd said about Jesus, and asked where we went to church in the UK, because he was currently living in Tooting, less than five minutes' walk from where Andy lived. Now, what are the chances of that happening?!

Pray for divine appointments and God will give them to you – but be ready to use them. Ananias was the only man who could speak to Saul, otherwise it wouldn't have tied in with his vision of '*a man named Ananias*' coming (v. 12). If Ananias had chickened out and sent his mate Keith or Barry instead to pray for Saul then it wouldn't have worked. Ananias was the only man for the job. Similarly, we are all in key positions with certain people. On a personal level, I can reach people that you can't. I've had opportunities to witness to a number of the UK's top 'adult' comedians, and seen one of them make a commitment to follow Jesus. You might feel totally inadequate and out of your depth about witnessing to people like this, but I feel at home and relaxed with them. However, I might feel equally uncomfortable trying to reach some of the individuals that you witness and relate to. I hope you can see what I'm getting at – we're all in unique positions with certain people.

Be friendly

Back to the story for the last time. I'm positive Ananias was quaking in his boots and filled with terror and fear as he made his way to his rendezvous with Saul in Straight Street. But the Bible tells us that his first words were friendly and welcoming: '*Brother Saul*' (v.17). It was Abraham Lincoln who said: '*Am I not destroying my enemies when I make friends of them?*' It's been said that kind words are music to a broken heart, and throughout the book we're going to be looking at the incredible effectiveness of friendship and being good news to those around us who don't yet know Jesus. But for now let me leave you with the true story of a great man of God, John Wesley, who showed friendliness and kindness in the face of extreme adversity.

As Wesley rode across Hounslow Heath late one night, singing hymns, he was startled by a fierce voice shouting, 'Halt,' while a hand seized the horse's bridle. The robber demanded, 'Your money or your life.' Wesley obediently emptied the few coins out of his pockets and invited the robber to examine his saddlebags, which were filled with books. Disappointed at the result, the robber was turning away when evangelist cried, 'Stop! I have something more to give you.'

The robber, wondering what he was talking about, turned back. Then Wesley, bending down toward him, said in solemn tones, 'My friend, you may live to regret the sort of a life in which you are engaged. If you ever do, I beseech you to remember this: the blood of Jesus Christ, God's Son, cleanseth us from all sin.' The robber hurried away, and Wesley rode off, praying in his heart that the words he had spoken might be remembered by the thief one day.

Years later, at the close of a Sunday church service, many people stayed behind to have a few words with the now elderly preacher, John Wesley. A stranger stepped forward and begged to speak with Mr Wesley. It was the robber of Hounslow Heath, now a successful businessman in the city, but now also a Christian. Wesley's words spoken that night long ago had been used by God in the man's conversion. Raising the hand of John Wesley to his lips, the former robber affectionately kissed it and said with deep emotion, 'To you, dear sir, I owe it all.' Wesley replied softly, 'Nay, nay, my friend, not to me, but to the precious blood of Christ, which cleanseth us from all sin.'

Boldness

I'm passionate about football and in particular my local team, Brighton and Hove Albion – pray for me now if you feel I need it! I find it dead easy talking to total strangers about their results and matches. I'm also passionate about Indian food. As a proud member of the Curry Club, I even write reports on restaurants that I visit. Once again, I find myself sharing my love and knowledge of curry with anyone, and indeed everyone, who is prepared to listen.

But often when it comes to Christianity and sharing Jesus with people, then it's easy to get a little 'hot under the collar' – and evangelism is my job! It's funny, isn't it? We find no problem in talking about the weather, or football, and what happened on *Coronation Street* last night, and other things that don't really matter. But when it comes to talking to unbelievers about important things, like our faith, then we start to panic a bit. I guess there are lots of reasons we're apprehensive, but maybe identifying the following eight might help us in increasing our boldness in our faith-sharing:

1 A fear of how people might react
2 We feel inadequate about sharing our faith
3 Worried about our lack of Bible knowledge
4 Not knowing what to say
5 We might be asked tough questions that we just can't answer
6 We feel we might do more harm than good

7   Worried of what people might think of us
8   A confused view of what evangelism and witnessing involve.

Well, the good news is that I'm going to be addressing all these issues later in this book. Let's start by looking at 'fear' which is the underlying concern for most of us, and see how we can start to overcome it and turn it into boldness.

Facing fear

Fear isn't just something that hinders Christians from getting on with their job. During the Second World War, a military governor met with the great General George Patton in Sicily. When the governor started praising him highly for his courage and fearlessness, Patton replied, '*Sir, I am not a brave man – the truth is, I am an utter coward. I have never been within the sound of gunshot or in the sight of battle in my whole life without being so scared that I had sweat in the palms of my hand.*' Years later, when Patton's autobiography was published, it contained a significant statement by the general: '*I learned very early on in my life never to take counsel of my fears.*'

One of my heroes, Billy Graham, admits his hands often go clammy and his knees shake before he preaches. Dr Graham once made a surprising admission:

> Every time I stand before a crowd I feel so unworthy to preach the gospel. I feel fearful that I may say something or do something that may mislead someone, because I'm talking to eternal souls, who have the possibility of living in heaven forever.

That's hardly a confession you would expect from a man who has preached the gospel to more people than anyone else in history. It is, however, a confession that should encourage us if we get nervous about sharing our faith with others.

Now let me take you back almost 2,000 years to Peter, one of Jesus' closest friends. This was the man who, on the night that Jesus died, denied three times that he even knew him. Yet, some weeks later, on the Day of Pentecost, he fearlessly preached the gospel and three thousand people became Christians.

Even the great apostle and evangelist, Paul, told the Christians in Corinth:

> I came to you in weakness and fear, and with much trembling. My message and my preaching were not with wise and persuasive words, but with a demonstration of the Spirit's power, so that your faith might not rest on men's wisdom, but on God's power. (1 Corinthians 2:3–5)

Most Christians feel fearful about evangelism; it really is perfectly normal to feel that way. But fear shouldn't disqualify us. Of course we'll get nervous and that can be a good thing. Nervousness tends to get the adrenaline flowing and helps you rely on God and pray more. I'm not talking about feeling nervous, but instead a fear that cripples you and stops you doing what God has in store for you; it almost creates a mindset that programmes you for failure.

Someone I know a lot about is Harry Houdini, the legendary escape artist who died in 1926. Houdini believed he was fearless and indeed invincible, and would issue an amazing challenge wherever he went. He could be locked in any jail cell in the country, he claimed, and would set himself free in a matter of minutes. Always he kept his promise, but one time something went badly wrong. Houdini entered the jail and the heavy, metal doors clanged shut behind him. He took from his belt a concealed piece of metal that was both strong and flexible to try to pick the lock. He set to work immediately, but something seemed to be unusual about this lock. For thirty minutes he worked and got nowhere. An hour passed, and still he had not opened the door. By now he was bathed in sweat and panting in exasperation, but he still couldn't pick the lock. Finally, after working away for two hours, the great Harry Houdini collapsed in frustration and failure against the door he couldn't unlock. But when he fell against the door, it swung open. It had never been locked at all. But in his mind it was locked, and that was all it took to keep him from opening the door and walking out of the jail cell.

Becoming bolder

The former American President Franklin D. Roosevelt said, '*The only thing we have to fear is fear itself.*' But fear can be overcome. In the New Testament, when the Holy Spirit came upon the disciples, God gave these once-timid men a great boldness. Bear in mind that these were the very same men who ran away and hid, devastated and demoralised after Jesus' death. The Gospel of John shows them huddled together in a room, locked away for fear of what their enemies would do to them.

It was into this setting that the resurrected Jesus came back and said: '*Peace be with you*' (John 20:19). After he had said this, he showed them his hands and side and proved to them that it was him and he had come back from the dead. Then he said it again:' "*Peace be with you! As the Father has sent me, I am sending you.*" *And with that he breathed on them and said, "Receive the Holy Spirit*" ' (John 20:21–2). The Holy Spirit changed these men and gave them great boldness.

The Greek word for 'boldness' here is *parrhesia*, which is an outspokenness and fearlessness that is a by-product of a person being filled with the Holy Spirit. If you're filled with the Holy Spirit, that boldness is available for you today, so let's take a look at a couple of principles to banish fear and give you this supernatural boldness.

Perfect love

The Bible tells us that the best antidote to fear is love.'*There is no fear in love. But perfect love drives out fear, because fear has to do with punishment. The one who fears is not made perfect in love*' (1 John 4:18). In 1988, I spent one of the best years of my life training on a Pioneer TIE (Training In Evangelism) team. I knew God had called me to be an evangelist, yet was one of the shyest people who you could care to meet. There was something deep within me that was desperate to proclaim the good news on the streets and in schools, but I was paralysed by fear. I was fearful of making mistakes and getting it wrong, what others might think of me, or just generally looking a complete idiot.

My discipler, Pete, with whom I spent the whole year training and travelling, prayed a great big dose of the love of God into my life – and it worked. Since that time I have had the great privilege of speaking to crowds of hundreds and even thousands at a time. The opportunities I have had on television, often on 'live' programmes, has enabled me to explain the gospel message to crowds of millions in one go. The love of God drives out all fear.

Pushing through pain barriers

At the end of the day, we need to be proactive when it comes to growing in boldness. I challenge you to take some risks in your evangelism, and God will show up.

I had an incredible time in Mexico City in 1998 when I was working with a small team. We happened to be there over the Hallowe'en period, which is a time of big occult activity through Mexico, when all the dead spirits are meant to come back to life on the 'Day of the Dead'. One afternoon we were meant to be doing an open-air presentation in a large park, right in the middle of this occult festival. A pretty bold thing to do, you might be thinking, but I felt God say that I should be on the main stage, not over in the corner of the park with a bunch of Christians armed with guitars, tracts and tambourines, where we had originally planned to do our presentation.

Well, would you believe it, that's what happened. I felt a bit nervous, but we went over and asked whether I could perform on the main stage. The organisers agreed, and thirty minutes later, yours truly ended up performing and preaching at the biggest occult festival in Central America, on stage with a coffin and an assortment of strange people in long black robes. After my gospel presentation, I invited the vast crowd to meet the 'Lord of Life' and over three hundred accepted Jesus. An evangelist speaking at an occult festival, what a wonderful irony!

It happened because when God opened a door of opportunity,

I decided, however fearful I felt, that I would push through and take full advantage of it. I hope it doesn't sound as if I'm bragging. Instead what I want to communicate is this. If God can use me, he can use anyone. And that includes you. Never forget, '*God did not give us a spirit of timidity, but a spirit of power, of love and of self-discipline*' (2 Timothy 1:7).

Communication

William Barclay was a well-known Scottish Bible scholar and preacher who died in February 1978. He once claimed that his unique ability to communicate the gospel so effectively was due to an old Scottish lady who lived alone in a tiny old house when he was a minister of Trinity Church in Renfrew. During a long illness one winter, Barclay visited her regularly until she recovered. On his last visit, she remonstrated, 'When you've been here, talking to me, and sometimes putting up a wee prayer, it's been grand, and I've understood every word you said. But man, when you're in yon pulpit on the Sabbath, you're awa' o'er ma head!' This encounter with a little old lady taught Barclay an important lesson that was to stick with him for the rest of his life.

Good communication is vital. The following comedy of errors actually appeared in a North American newspaper several years ago.

First Day: FOR SALE – R. D. Jones has one sewing-machine for sale. Phone 958-3030 after 7 p.m. and ask for Mrs Kelly who lives with him cheap.

The next day the advertisement was 'corrected' to read:

NOTICE – We regret having erred in R. D. Jones' advertisement yesterday. It should have read: 'One sewing-machine for sale. Cheap. Phone 958-3030 and ask for Mrs Kelly who lives with him after 7 p.m.'

That correction was 'corrected' the day after. It read:

> R. D. Jones has informed us that he has received several anonymous telephone calls because of the error we made in his classified ad yesterday. His ad stands corrected as follows: 'FOR SALE – R. D. Jones has one sewing-machine for sale. Cheap. Phone 958-3030 after 7 p.m. and ask for Mrs Kelly who loves with him.'

Finally, the day after, Mr Jones 'corrected' the ad himself with a further ad:

> NOTICE – I, R. D. Jones, have no sewing-machine for sale. I SMASHED IT. Don't call 958-3030 as the telephone has been taken out. I have not been carrying on with Mrs Kelly. Until yesterday she was my housekeeper, but SHE QUIT!

A bit far-fetched perhaps, but I'm told it really did happen. Poor communication led to total confusion, and in this case, one smashed-up sewing-machine as well! The Greeks said that really effective communication had three qualities: *ethos*, *pathos* and *logia*.

- *Ethos* is the root word for 'ethics' – a set of moral principles. As Christians we must be a good example in our words and actions. If our lifestyle doesn't match up to our words then we are hypocrites.
- *Pathos* is the root of 'sympathy' and 'empathy'. A good moral person who lacks compassion (*pathos*) can be as hard as a rock and cold as ice. Care, compassion and empathy, therefore, are vital parts of communication.
- *Logia* translates into 'word' – the content of what we say. At the end of the day we can be the most upright and caring people in the world and others think we're wonderful, but they are unlikely to ever become Christians if they don't hear the gospel message.

Good communication involves all the three aspects intertwined. Throughout this book we're going to be looking at many different forms of communicating the gospel, with I hope helpful techniques and frameworks through which the Holy Spirit can move. Let's start by going back to basics and looking at how God communicated 2,000 years ago by becoming one of us, in the form of Jesus.

Forget the image of a wimp in a nightie and instead picture a thirty-year-old Jewish man, surrounded by twelve friends and a crowd of adults and children, some listening, others mocking and heckling. It would have been hot, crowded and sandy, yet this man had the ability to capture and hold their attention with storytelling, laced with humour and compassion. He made the time to talk to restless toddlers sitting on his lap and crooked taxmen up trees, and everyone, so it seemed, in between. When he told stories he filled them with visual aids, jokes and drama that people could relate to. He made them chuckle, so it would make it easier for them to remember. It seems from reading the Bible, he managed to communicate with everyone he met – whatever their age or level of understanding – and pointed them to his heavenly Father.

The apostle Paul also seemed to be prepared to go to almost any length to enter the world of unbelievers and lead them to Jesus:

> Though I am free and belong to no man, I make myself a slave to everyone, to win as many as possible. To the Jews I became like a Jew, to win the Jews. To those under the law I became like one under the law (though I myself am not under the law), so as to win those under the law. To those not having the law I became like one not having the law (though I am not free from God's law but am under Christ's law), so as to win those not having the law. To the weak I became weak, to win the weak. I have become all things to all men so that by all possible means I might save some. I do all this for the sake of the gospel, that I may share in its blessings. (1 Corinthians 9:19–23)

To me, that seems to be a fantastic manifesto for communication. But how do we become '*all things to all men*'? Let me make a few suggestions.

Listen

Franklin D. Roosevelt got tired of smiling and saying the usual things at White House receptions during his presidential term of office. So, one evening he decided to find out whether anybody was paying attention to what he was saying. As each person came up to him with extended hand, he flashed a big smile and said, 'I murdered my grandmother this morning.' People would automatically respond with comments such as 'How lovely!' or 'Just continue with your great work!' Nobody listened to what he was saying, except one foreign diplomat. When the president said, 'I murdered my grandmother this morning', the diplomat responded softly, 'I'm sure she had it coming to her.'

We need to become better listeners. Remember: we have two ears and one mouth that we may listen more and talk less. Don't talk about yourself all the time. Instead, listen, be sincere and show an interest in what the other person is saying as well as listening to what God has to say about the person.

Connect

You are the human link between God and the person, so connect with them. When I'm witnessing I try to find some common ground with the person, so we can connect and engage. Be enthusiastic and find where they're coming from, which of course shouldn't be too hard if you've already listened carefully to them. Don't talk at them, talk with them and adapt your conversation to them personally.

A little while ago, I was involved with a mission in Dorset with a well-respected, senior evangelist. A drama company and I were involved with the youth work, visiting schools to invite teenagers to a Friday night youth event. The evangelist insisted on speaking to the crowd, but I have to say he didn't connect with his youthful audience. As part of his talk, he told the old story about the Wellington flying over the Swiss Alps during the Second World War. You probably know the one. The plane was running out of fuel and the padre in the back was dumping all the ballast to help the plane clear the mountain-tops. There was still too much weight in the plane, so the padre jumped out and sacrificed his life so the plane and its crew would survive. Now I have to say that's a great story and has a tremendous gospel application, but the teenagers in Wimborne that night were scratching their heads wondering what a Wellington *boot* – the speaker hadn't explained that it was a Wellington *bomber* – was doing flying in Switzerland. He had failed to connect with them.

Words

Mark Twain, on his return from France, said: '*In Paris they simply stared when I spoke to them in French; I never did succeed in making those idiots understand their own language.*' Many Christians seem to develop a strange religious language soon after they become Christians, so when you're communicating to unbelievers make your language understandable and jargon-free. Jesus used parables – simple stories and illustrations that people today would understand. If he were around today he would probably tell stories about *EastEnders*, Playstation 2, Manchester United and the Internet. He used his stories to make the truth easier to understand and harder to forget. It should be the same with our communication.

And do be enthusiastic. Christians should be the happiest and most enthusiastic people on the face of the earth. Indeed, the actual word 'enthusiasm' comes from the Greek word, *entheous*, which literally means 'full of God'. A smile will break the ice and your enthusiasm for what you're sharing can be infectious. After all, the message we have to share is 'good news'.

Challenge

It's wonderful to be 'salt and light' with our friends and in our communities, but we do need to mention Jesus as well, otherwise we'll become just nice people or do-gooders. Never be afraid to be up-front about why Jesus came and died and rose again to give us all new life. Challenge your listener to take things further. There's an ancient Chinese proverb that says: '*To talk much and arrive nowhere is the same as climbing a tree to catch a fish.*' It might not be terribly British to challenge a person to make a decision. Well, so what? If we're going to win people for Jesus then I think it's time to stop being so British and start being more like Jesus. He was never afraid to challenge people, even though they didn't always feel ready to count the cost of following him. When I challenge people, I tend to ask open-ended questions. By that I mean questions that they have to answer by saying more than just 'yes' or 'no'.

In personal witnessing after a great conversation, where I've listened, engaged and talked about Christianity, I often ask: 'Why don't you become a Christian now?' You've got nothing to lose by asking this. Some people aren't ready, but many of them are and I have had the wonderful privilege of leading many of them to Jesus. Don't feel threatened yourself by this vital step in communication. Go on, give it a go!

Demonstrate

It's said that when St Francis of Assisi had finished preparing his disciples for their work of evangelising the world, he gave one more surprising instruction. When motivating and inspiring them to communicate the gospel, he reminded them that it would not simply be the words they spoke that would reveal the heart of their message: '*If you have to, use words.*' St Francis knew that the most powerful sign would be for his disciples' lives and actions to communicate their message.

Your life will communicate more than your words ever do, so '*walk the talk*'. When H. M. Stanley went to Africa in 1871 to find and report on David Livingstone, he spent several months in the missionary's company, carefully observing the man and his work. Apparently Livingstone never spoke to Stanley about God and Christianity, but Livingstone's loving and patient compassion for the African people was beyond Stanley's comprehension. He just couldn't understand how the missionary could have such love for and patience with the backward, pagan people among whom he had been ministering for years. Stanley wrote in his journal, 'When I saw that unwearied patience, that unflagging zeal, and those enlightened sons of Africa, I became a Christian at his side, though he never spoke to me one word.'

Door to Door

Hands up, I have to admit that I really don't enjoy doing door-to-door work one little bit. Give me the opportunity to speak to a thousand rowdy teenagers in a Monday morning school assembly and you'll see me rubbing my hands together with glee. Yet those very same hands are shaking with trepidation when I know I have to do some door-to-door work, and I guess I'm not alone.

Certainly in Britain, '*an Englishman's home is his castle*', or so the old saying goes, and we can feel it's a bit of an affront to turn up on a complete stranger's doorstep with a message which, we may feel, they don't really want to hear. However, as your average person sees no need to go to church, we need to think about going to them. Visiting house to house is a good way of doing that – if we do it the right way.

Goals

It always helps to have a clearly defined purpose, and something your whole church can own and really get behind. After all, if you have nothing to aim at, you're never going to hit anything. So let's think about what your goals should be on the doors:

Prayer-walking

I'm not talking about a full blown praise march here with banners, guitars and a portable amplifier blasting out the latest 'Now that's what I call Graham Kendrick 42' CD. Instead I'm talking about going out in pairs, simply walking and praying over the streets you're going to be visiting in the days and weeks to come. Pray for a softening of hearts and that you will be well received.

Introduction to your church

You might decide your goal is to raise the profile of your church. I always feel it is good to leave something at every home, so leave a brochure about the church with all its latest exciting news. Of course this needs to be written and presented in a way that is attractive and seeker-sensitive. Get rid of all the in-jokes and religious jargon, or you'll be wasting your money.

Invitation to a special event

It could be that your church is running a special event, or even better a series of events that you want unbelievers to come to. It could be a series of special guest meetings for the whole family, on the first Sunday of each month, for example. It might be in the run-up to a school holiday where your church is running a children's club, this will be a tremendous blessing for many a parent! Or you might be relaunching an *Alpha* course, or running a series of evangelistic meals with well-known speakers. Going on the doors is a wonderful way to advertise your event to hundreds of unsaved people.

Surveys

There are two types of surveys that I have used that have worked well. At no extra expense I have reproduced them in the Appendixes at the back of the book. How about that for value for money?!

Appendix 1 is a Community Survey, which basically assesses the needs of folk in the community, and asks how as a church you might be able to be part of the answer. The second appendix, which is more up-front in terms of gospel content, is a Beliefs Questionnaire, which asks questions about the person's beliefs. The last question is always: 'If it was possible to have a personal relationship with God, would you be interested?' When they say 'yes', and many people do, this might, if it is appropriate, be the time to lead them to Christ.

Offer prayer

Believe me, people really appreciate this, particularly senior citizens, as you offer to pray for them, their families and situations. If they don't want prayer then and there, then ask if you can pray for them through the week. They will rarely refuse, and of course it gives you the opportunity to go back to see if your prayer has been answered.

Relationships

The key on the doors is always building relationships. Whether you've targeted an entire estate, or just one road, it's individuals that matter and that's what counts. In a matter of minutes you can smash several of the stereotypes that many people have about Christians and Christianity, as long as you leave your tambourines and sandals at home! Just be good news and show how normal, yet different, Christians are.

Timing

This is going to affect what personnel are able to be part of your team. There are, of course, pros and cons for each of these:

- Daytime is good for mums with young children, the unemployed, housebound and retired people – though many other people will be out at work.
- Early evening – most people are around in the early evening. Be aware of interrupting meals and children's bedtimes.
- Saturdays – most office workers have a day off on Saturday. Don't go too early and disturb well-deserved lie-ins, and be aware that lots of people will be out shopping or out with the children.
- Sunday mornings – obviously the best time to catch people

who don't go to church, but you can receive an unwelcoming response if you get people out of bed on their day off.

Return visits

As was said earlier, the key should always be the building of relationships. Relationships take time, so build into your door-to-door strategy a series of repeat visits. Let me give you an example of a twelve-month strategy that results in four visits:

- Winter – in the lead up to Christmas, people are used to unbidden callers coming to their doors anyway, mainly the carol-singing variety who expect money. Why not really surprise those you visit with a Christmas card, a free mince pie and an invitation to your church's Christmas activities?
- Spring – your second visit is just before Easter. This time you return with a Cadbury's Cream Egg and an invitation to your Easter Sunday guest service.
- Summer – you return in the early summer with an invitation to your church barbecue, with another free gift, this time a voucher for a free hot dog when they come along.
- Autumn – the fourth visit of the year, is with an invitation to a meal – harvest or otherwise. This sort of event might include an after-dinner speaker who will communicate the Christian message in an entertaining and relevant way. Of course the invitation contains a voucher entitling them to 50 per cent discount off the ticket price.

Prayer

Once again, with all evangelistic endeavours, prayer should always be the backbone of all we do. It was the great preacher Charles Spurgeon who said, '*I would rather teach one man to pray, than ten men to preach.*' Prayer changes things, there's no doubt about it. Every time half your team is out on the streets, make sure the other half are praying specifically for the homes, streets and individuals that will be visited. The next time, reverse the roles, so everyone enjoys (and they will enjoy it) being part of the overall strategy of reaching your neighbourhood with the good news.

Evangelists

When the evangelist D. L. Moody was conducting evangelistic meetings, he frequently faced hecklers. In the final service of one of his crusades, an usher handed the famous American preacher a note as he entered the auditorium. It was actually from an atheist who had been giving Mr Moody a great deal of trouble throughout the gospel campaign. The evangelist, however, thought that it was an announcement, so he asked the large audience to be quiet as he prepared to read it along with the other notices. Opening the folded piece of paper he found scrawled in large print only one word: 'Fool!' The preacher was equal to the occasion. Said Moody, 'I have just been handed a letter which contains the single word, "Fool". This is most unusual. I've often heard of those who have written letters and forgotten to sign their names, but this is the first time I've ever heard of anyone who signed his name and then forgot to write the letter!' Taking advantage of the unique situation, Moody promptly changed his sermon text to Psalm 14:1: 'The fool says in his heart, "There is no God."' How about that for quick thinking?

I don't know what mental picture is conjured up in your mind by the word 'evangelist'. I guess for the majority of our unbelieving friends it might be that of an immaculately dressed American telly evangelist, with super shiny teeth and perfectly coiffured hairstyle. He'll probably be preaching in a vast auditorium, surrounded by a massed choir, while pulling on the heart-strings and appealing for money. He may remind them of Steve Martin as the con-man evangelist from the movie *Leap of Faith*.

For others, it could be an image of a scruffy old man with an unkempt beard, sandals and a long coat, wearing a sandwich board emblazoned with an obscure Old Testament verse. He'll also have a regulation black leather-bound Bible and an exhaustive range of gospel tracts bulging out of every pocket. He'll be ready with a Bible verse for every possible situation, and is likely to resemble a cross between a walking Christian bookshop and a flasher! A friend of mine encountered such a character while shopping in Chichester one Saturday. The man in question was shouting at passers-by that they were going to hell. He spotted my friend Jeff and bellowed at him: 'Are you going to heaven?' To which Jeff replied, 'No, Tesco' and hurried off!

The actual Greek word *evangelist*, interestingly enough, originally wasn't even a spiritual word as such. It was the word applied to certain slaves in wartime whose assignment it was to serve alongside an army general. If their side won, the slave's task would be to run with the news of his general's victory. It's not too hard to imagine the families back home worrying about their men fighting in battle, but when they saw the evangelist coming towards them, they knew the battle was won. The arrival of the evangelist always preceded the arrival of the winning army, and his news prepared the people for their victory celebrations.

Perhaps a modern understanding of the word 'evangelist' is a person, called of God, who enjoys evangelism and is good at actually doing it, and training others to do it. While writing to the church in Ephesus, Paul described the role of an evangelist like this:

> It was he who gave some to be apostles, some to be prophets, some to be evangelists, and some to be pastors and teachers, to prepare God's people for works of service, so that the body of Christ may be built up until we all reach unity in the faith and in the knowledge of the Son of God and become mature, attaining

to the whole measure of the fullness of Christ. (Ephesians 4:11–13)

It couldn't be clearer really – the function of the evangelist is to equip the Church for evangelism. He or she is not just someone who does it, but also equips, prepares and enables others to do it too.

So that's what an evangelist is. Let's now take a closer look at the word '*evangelism*'. It literally means 'good news', but is not a word that is used in the Bible. Indeed the word 'evangelist' only appears three times in the entire Bible:

1   Philip was called to be an evangelist. '*Leaving the next day, we reached Caesarea and stayed at the house of Philip the evangelist, one of the Seven*' (Acts 21:8).
2   Timothy was called to do the work of an evangelist. '*But you, keep your head in all situations, endure hardship, do the work of an evangelist, discharge all the duties of your ministry*' (2 Timothy 4:5).
3   Paul describes the evangelist, as we've seen already, as one of the gifts Jesus had given the Church. '*It was he who gave some to be . . . evangelists . . . to prepare God's people for works of service*' (Ephesians 4:11).

Having said all of the above, the verb form of the word *euangelion* appears again and again, fifty-two times to be absolutely precise, and simply means to 'proclaim the good news'. The angels did it when they told people about Jesus' birth: '*But the angel said to them, "Do not be afraid. I bring you good news of great joy that will be for all the people"* ' (Luke 2:10).

Later, Jesus proclaimed the 'evangel' of the kingdom of God: '*After John was put in prison, Jesus went into Galilee, proclaiming the good news of God. "The time has come," he said. "The kingdom of God is near. Repent and believe the good news!"* ' (Mark 1:14–15). These are just two of the examples; maybe have a go at finding the other fifty yourself. By using verbs – doing words – when it talks about evangelism, the Bible couldn't make it more obvious that evangelism is about action – actually doing it.

Research tells us that around 10 per cent of Christians have evangelism as their main gift, so you probably don't need a university degree in mathematics to figure out that about 90 per cent of Christians aren't evangelists. You may be heaving a massive sigh of relief at this point, but this doesn't mean you can opt out of sharing your faith. Apart from the fact that it's brilliant fun, the Bible says we're all witnesses, without exception: '*But you will receive power when the Holy Spirit comes on you; and you will be my witnesses in Jerusalem, and in all Judea and Samaria, and to the ends of the earth*' (Acts 1:8).

I don't know if you've ever been to court. I have, and I found the whole process rather nerve-racking to say the least. So much so, I dropped all my well-prepared papers all over the floor of the courtroom and the poor clerk of the court was scrabbling around on the floor trying to pick up my sheaves of copious notes. Still, it got a bit of a laugh from the magistrates and eased the tension somewhat. But anyway, my task on that day as a witness was to tell the magistrates what happened to me and what I had seen and experienced. And that is the job of a witness, to tell others what has happened to them. Of course the $64,000 question is: Are you a good witness, or a bad witness?

The New Testament word for witness is *martus*, from which we get the English word 'martyr', someone who is put to death for refusing to renounce a faith or belief. Now don't panic! We might not have to physically lay down our lives for Jesus and the gospel, but we may need to lay down other things for him as we strive to reach others.

It could be that we need to sacrifice more time for our neighbours, or actually be prepared to give our money to invest in evangelism. It might be that we need to go out of our way to share the gospel at times when we don't feel like doing it because it's simply not terribly convenient. Giving costs, but Jesus promises to give back much, much more:

> I tell you the truth, unless a grain of wheat falls to the ground and dies, it remains only a single seed. But if it dies, it produces many seeds. The man who loves his life will lose it, while the man who hates his life in this world will

keep it for eternal life. Whoever serves me must follow me; and where I am, my servant also will be. My Father will honour the one who serves me. (John 12:24–6)

Friendship

'*Now the tax collectors and "sinners" were all gathering around to hear him. But the Pharisees and the teachers of the law muttered, "This man welcomes sinners and eats with them"*' (Luke 15:1–2). Jesus was a friend of 'sinners' – he consistently went out of his way to spend time with and befriend them. It was the great English preacher, Charles Spurgeon, who said: '*Friendship is one of the sweetest joys of life. Many might have failed beneath the bitterness of their trial had they not found a friend.*' Pretty profound, so allow me to ask you ten questions:

1 Are you friendly?
2 Do you know the names of your next-door neighbours?
3 Are you good news?
4 Do you have many Christian friends?
5 More importantly, do you have many non-Christian friends?
6 Do you see your neighbours more than once a week?
7 Have you ever invited your neighbours to your home for a drink or a meal?
8 Do you make an effort to make friends at all?
9 Would you notice if your neighbours were away from home?
10 In an emergency would you ask your friends or neighbours for help?

I wonder how you did in that quick test. Maybe you are civil to your neighbours, attend family reunions and just about get on with work colleagues, but none of that is the hallmark of true friendship. Australian scientist Thomas Hughes hit the nail on the head when he said:

> Blessed are they who have the gift of making friends, for it is one of God's best gifts. It involves many things, but above all, the power of going out of one's self and appreciating whatever is noble and loving in another.

Friendships and relationships are vitally important to God. In the beginning, in Eden when God created the world – and in it man – there was still something that was not quite right. There was something missing. God and Adam was not enough; Adam needed friendship with other human beings, so God created Eve, the missing piece of the puzzle. Quite simply, humankind was made for friendship and relationships.

Friendship is also the most effective form of evangelism. A major survey was taken in the early 1980s when 10,000 people were asked the question: 'What was responsible for you coming to Christ and this church?' The results make for very interesting reading:

Evangelistic crusades	0.5	%
Organised visitation	1	%
Special need	2	%
Just walked in	3	%
Special event	3	%
Sunday school	3	%
Pastoral contact	6	%
Friend or relative	79	%

Source: The Institute of Church Growth, Pasadena, California

Although it's been twenty years or so since the original statistics were formulated, the Church Growth Institute have formulated similar figures with groups in hundreds of seminars, and the numbers still hold true today:

Advertisement	2	%
Organised visitation	6	%
Pastoral contact	6	%
Friend or relative	86	%

These figures should have tremendous implications for all Christians. They show clearly that friendships and relationships appear to be the best way of reaching the lost. If we want to change the world we must live in the world. To the men reading this who are desperate to reach their mates at the pub on a Sunday night, you aren't going to do it by sitting at home drinking cocoa and watching reruns of *Songs of Praise*. We must get out of our cosy Christian lives, and start making an effort to make friends and start being good news.

It's funny, isn't it, when it comes to evangelism most of us try the difficult things first: door-to-door work, stopping people in the street to give them a gospel tract, or singing cheesy Christian folk songs outside Sainsbury's and getting in everyone's way on a busy Saturday afternoon. A few knock-backs or bad experiences can be pretty soul-destroying and can sometimes put Christians off doing evangelism altogether. However, inviting your neighbours round, or taking them out for a drink, or going to see a movie with them is a different matter altogether, and can bring a completely different response. You might actually enjoy it and want to do it again, so that can't be bad, can it?!

It was Dale Carnegie, an American author and psychologist, who said this about friendships: '*You can make more friends in two months by becoming really interested in other people than you can in two years trying to get other people interested in you.*' This is another way of saying that the best way to make a friend is to be a friend. We all need friends, and as we spend time with them, talking about what they find important, it gives us a very natural right to share what matters to us.

Here are my ten top tips (and that's not easy to say in a hurry!) on how to be a better friend. I'll be unpacking most of the principles later on in this book, but here are some ideas, thoughts and suggestions to whet your appetite in the meantime:

Quality time

You get to know someone by spending time with them so, first and foremost, choose to invest quality time with your friends. I'll be perhaps a tad controversial here, and suggest you should maybe drop a church activity or two, or even stop spending so much time with your Christian friends, to befriend the lost. Choose things to do that you'll know you'll both enjoy. If you can't swim, don't suggest you should swim the English Channel while greased up with lard one afternoon. Instead share common interests.

For me that means prioritising an evening a week for a boys' night at our local sports and social club. Every Sunday, almost without fail, from 9 p.m. you'll find us enjoying a few pints, having a laugh and talking about everything under the sun. Then in the week if there seems to be a good football match in prospect, the lads will come round to my home and we'll watch the game together. At other times, we get together with our wives for a meal, and often we'll do something all together with our children: a walk in the country, a barbecue, swimming or flying kites down the beach. We went on holiday with our neighbours – even sharing a caravan for good measure. It was a blast!

Prayer

Prayer is the secret ingredient in evangelism. I'm going to be saying a lot more about prayer later on in the book. Martin Luther said, '*As it is the business of tailors to make clothes and of cobblers to mend shoes, so it is the business of Christians to pray.*' Our prayers make all the difference, so let's be specific and focused.

For our neighbours, Scott and Martine, there have been at least three occasions where God has intervened in quite dramatic ways. First, Martine encountered problems during pregnancy; then when baby Louis was finally born his arm was dislocated and the nerves in his arm were badly damaged. Third, we prayed for the healing of their niece, who was critically injured in a horrendous road accident. Her condition seemed so desperate, she was even administered the last rites.

God stepped into each of these situations in remarkable ways. Martine gave birth safely; a paediatric consultant has said Louis's arm is perfect and he no longer needs any physiotherapy or other treatment; and their niece is home from hospital and making a remarkable recovery. Isn't God good?

Introduce them to your Christian friends

It's important to choose the right ones here. During a boys' night out at our local curry house the other week, one of my Christian friends asked my mate Bruno what he thought about judgement and eternal damnation. Definitely not the most sensitive thing to ask on a low-key night out, while enjoying a glass of wine and a chicken vindaloo. Poor old Bruno almost choked on his chapatti!

I'm absolutely convinced that half the battle here is showing unbelievers that Christians aren't all wallies in flares, sandals and beards – and that's just the women! Joking aside, let's show them we're ordinary people who have met God in an extraordinary way.

Tell your story

We'll see later how effective your personal story can be. When you've earned the right to do so, start to share your experiences of how God helps you through life, and how you met him for yourself. Done naturally, this will be very normal and could have an incredible effect.

A missionary in India was once teaching the Bible to a group of Hindu women. Halfway through the lesson, one of them got up and walked out. A short time later, she came back and listened more intently than ever. At the close of the hour the leader enquired, 'Why did you leave the meeting? Weren't you interested?'

'Oh yes,' the Hindu lady replied. 'I was so impressed with what you had to say about Christ that I went out to ask your driver whether you really lived the way you talked. When he said you did, I hurried back so I wouldn't miss out on anything.'

Your story and life will speak volumes.

Invite them to events

Once again, think about this carefully. Unfortunately, your average Sunday meeting might not be the best thing to invite your friend to. So it might be best to wait for the monthly guest meeting, where things are especially geared for outsiders. Christmas and Easter are times that more people go to church, so that might be more appropriate. If that's still not suitable, something less threatening like a meal or other social event could be just the occasion for your friend to meet more Christians, enjoy themselves and hear more about Christianity. More about suitable events is coming up later.

What do they need from you?

Have a good think about what your friends might need from you. By that I mean it could be emotional support or they might need more practical help. Maybe it's an elderly neighbour you could cook for, or just visit or invite in for a chat and a cup of tea. A while ago, a new couple moved into our street, so we bought them a bottle of wine and a card, which my wife took over. They were absolutely bowled over as no one had ever done anything like that before.

The women in our church are great when it comes to a mum, be she part of our church or not, giving birth. Straightaway someone draws up a rota, and that family is delivered a good, hot meal every day for at least a week. You wouldn't believe the impact it can have on the rest of the neighbourhood when they see a steady stream of meals arriving every night at teatime. Once again, it gives a very natural and normal reason to explain our motivation for doing it.

Listen to them

Two men were talking one day. One of them said, 'My wife talks to herself a lot.'

His friend answered, 'Mine does, too, but she doesn't know it. She thinks I'm listening.'

Communication is a vital way of building a good friendship, though once again bear in mind the profound words of the Greek philosopher Diogenes: '*We have two ears and one mouth that we may listen the more and talk the less.*'

Listen to your friends and don't talk about yourself all the time – it can be so irritating. It drives me up the wall, and I tend to call it the 'taxi-driver mentality'. Apologies to all taxi-drivers out there who aren't like this, but most of those I've encountered are the kind of people who, if you've got a black cat, then they'll own a panther called Shadow! They tend to be the world's biggest experts on everything. Do you know the sort of people I mean? No one likes a know-it-all, so don't talk about yourself all the time. Don't even talk about the Lord all the time (I'm sure he won't mind). Don't come up with all the right answers. Trust me, your friends won't appreciate it. Instead listen to them, and think about how Jesus can help them.

Be honest about yourself

While thinking about this point I was reminded of the story of a minister who was trying to say in his Sunday sermon that none of us is perfect and, not only that, none of us today even has the opportunity of knowing a perfect person. In fact, he went so far as to challenge the people, asking them if any of them had even heard of a perfect person. He was understandably surprised when one man actually stood up and stated that he knew of such a person. The dumbfounded vicar asked him for details: Did he really know him? Had he met him? The man admitted that he didn't know the man personally, but he had certainly heard a great deal about him. In fact, this legendary man of many perfections was his wife's first husband.

None of us is perfect, so let's be honest about our failures and confide, where appropriate, in our friends. But also share your dreams and aspirations as well as enjoying telling them how God has answered your prayers.

Be patient

They do say that the average person, if there is such a thing, has to hear the gospel seven times before they make a decision to follow Christ. So be patient. A little tip here: It's sometimes easier to have patience with others when we remember God's patience toward us, so remember that when you get particularly impatient and frustrated.

Some years ago, Dr James Engel, a marketing professor at Ohio State University, developed a scale which looks at the process a person goes through on the road to knowing Jesus and becoming a disciple. Now I know what you're thinking, God doesn't have to work to scales or diagrams. Absolutely true. But this scale might be helpful in seeing how the good news can work, and where your friend might be on their journey to faith in Christ.

-8 Awareness of Supreme Being
-7 Initial awareness of the gospel
-6 Awareness of the fundamentals of the gospel
-5 A grasp of the implications of the gospel
-4 Positive attitude towards the gospel
-3 A recognition of personal problems
-2 Decision to do something about it
-1 Repentance and new faith in Jesus
NEW CREATION
+1 Evaluation of decision
+2 Integration into the church
+3 Conceptual and behavioural growth
+4 Communion with God
+5 Active in evangelism.

Bear this journey in mind when you're feeling impatient.

Remember the Dutch proverb: '*A handful of patience is worth more than a bushel of brains.*' Keep going and keep praying and ask God for breakthrough.

Enjoy it

The problem with producing lists is that some people think they're some sort of magic formula. Friendship isn't a formula; it's a natural process that should be great fun. Over the years I've spent a lot of time with friends eating at my local Indian restaurant, and in time getting to know the staff and management as well. Indeed, so well that I now count them as friends. When Jemma, my wife, and I got married we invited a contingent from Tandoori Nights to join us and celebrate our big day with us.

I've got to say I was dead chuffed to see the manager, Mr Miah, and his family turn up, and was intrigued by the two huge presents he struggled through the doors with. It was the first Christian meeting they'd ever been to and they loved it. As a mark of their friendship they had bought us a barbecue and a microwave oven. We were so touched. Six years later, Mr Miah and the gang at Tandoori Nights aren't saved, but I firmly believe they're all a little further down the road, and that's the very nature of what friendship evangelism is all about – making friends and bringing people closer to Jesus.

I get misunderstood and criticised by people in the church I go to for having a few pints, but I don't care one bit. I've already mentioned our boys' get-togethers on Sundays. Well, we baptised our first two members last week. Isn't that fantastic? Our neighbours, Scott and Martine, have become two of our closest friends and their son classes my wife, our children and myself as part of his family. Christian friends are wonderful and very important but just think of all the other friends you could have if you looked out of church and instead looked at those around you. You too could probably have wonderful neighbours like ours.

Let's finish this chapter with one last quote, this time from Indian Yogi, Paramahansa Yogananda: '*There is a magnet in your heart that will attract true friends. That magnet is unselfishness, thinking of others first . . . when you learn to live for others, they will live for you.'*

E-H

Gospel

We saw in the first chapter how Saul was converted and became Paul the great missionary. After his dramatic conversion he preached the gospel boldly all over Jerusalem. When the Jews there tried to kill him, the other Christians smuggled him safely out of the city, took him to Caesarea and then on to his home-town of Tarsus. In the years that followed, Paul escaped death frequently. Once an angry mob tried to stone him and his colleague Barnabas while in Iconium, but they were able to escape to Lystra. Another time, the Jews from Iconium who were chasing Paul and Barnabas turned a crowd against these men of God. They stoned Paul and dragged him out of the city, leaving him for dead. But as the disciples gathered around him, Paul was miraculously able to stand and walked back into the city.

Time and time again, Paul was caught and imprisoned, and again and again he escaped. He was thrown in prison in Philippi; then in the middle of the night God sent an earthquake which caused the prison doors to open and Paul's chains to fall off. Between terms of imprisonment en route to Rome to be tried before Caesar, he survived a shipwreck only to be bitten by a deadly poisonous snake. Paul simply shook the snake off into the fire, preached the gospel, and many people became Christians.

In a letter to the church in Corinth, Paul gave an account of his suffering:

I have worked much harder, been in prison more frequently, been flogged more severely, and been exposed to death again and again. Five times I received from the Jews the forty lashes minus one. Three times I was beaten with rods, once I was stoned, three times I was shipwrecked, I spent a night and a day in the open sea, I have been constantly on the move. I have been in danger from rivers, in danger from bandits, in danger from my own countrymen, in danger from Gentiles; in danger in the city, in danger in the country, in danger at sea; and in danger from false brothers. I have laboured and toiled and have often gone without sleep; I have known hunger and thirst and have often gone without food; I have been cold and naked. (2 Corinthians 11:23–7)

After further missionary journeys, Paul was eventually arrested again for what was to be the last time, as by now being a follower of Jesus carried the death penalty. As his execution drew near, he wrote to his friend Timothy:

I have fought the good fight, I have finished the race, I have kept the faith. Now there is in store for me the crown of righteousness, which the Lord, the righteous Judge, will award to me on that day. (2 Timothy 4:7–8)

This awesome man of God was finally beheaded in Rome, in around AD 65.

Paul had met Jesus, fallen in love with him and dedicated his life to telling others the glorious message of the gospel. To Paul, the gospel wasn't just a nice theory or technique that got people saved. No, it was a powerful truth and a reason for glory. A cause so great he was prepared to lay his life down for it.

This is what he said about the gospel:

I am bound both to Greeks and non-Greeks, both to the wise and the foolish. That is why I am so eager to preach the gospel also to you who are at Rome. I am not ashamed of the gospel, because it is the power of God for the salvation of everyone who believes: first for the Jew, then for the Gentile. For in the gospel a righteousness from God is revealed, a righteousness that is by faith from first to last, just as it is written: 'The righteous will live by faith.' (Romans 1:14–17)

Paul was consumed by sharing the gospel, and we should be too. What we have to communicate to a needy world is not merely good advice and helpful suggestions; it is good news that changes lives. Good news is infectious, you just can't help telling others. When each of my children was born, even though it was the middle of the night, I just had to phone all my friends and tell them. It would have been selfish not to have told others, and to have kept it to ourselves. As the old saying goes, '*Unshared joy is like an unlighted candle.*'

In the same way, Jesus never intended that we should keep the good news of the gospel to ourselves. The word *gospel* literally means 'good news', and just as Jesus was sent to earth by his Father, so he sent his disciples, '*As the Father has sent me, I am sending you*' (John 20:21). And we in turn have to take this message to those who have not yet heard this good news. The gospel needs to be proclaimed and something happens when we start to do it, as God backs up our words.

The gospel has many different facets and is described in many different ways throughout the Bible. We're told it's the good news of salvation, reconciliation, peace and hope.

Salvation

'*And you also were included in Christ when you heard the word of truth, the gospel of your salvation*' (Ephesians 1:13). Salvation through Jesus brings a deliverance, a rescue and general wellbeing. The original Greek word *soteria* is used both in a material sense as well as a spiritual sense.

Reconciliation

'*This mystery is that through the gospel the Gentiles are heirs together with Israel, members together of one body, and sharers together in the promise in Christ Jesus*' (Ephesians 3:6). Paul here is reflecting on the mission of the good news to help believing Jews and Gentiles accept each other as partners in God's promise of salvation. This 'mystery' was particularly foreign to the Old Testament Jewish mindset, which was understood by neither Jew or Gentile until Jesus came.

Peace

'*And with your feet fitted with the readiness that comes from the gospel of peace*' (Ephesians 6:15). At the time of writing this letter, Paul may have been chained by the wrist to a Roman soldier and he would have seen a ready-made picture of a Christian wearing his armour, ready to do the work of God. The soldier's sandals were the sign of one equipped and ready to move. Let's be ready to move and eager to share the message of the gospel with others who haven't heard it, whenever and wherever we can.

Hope

If you continue in your faith, established and firm, not moved from the hope held out in the gospel. This is the gospel that you heard and that has been proclaimed to every creature under heaven, and of which I, Paul, have become a servant. (Colossians 1:23)

Knowing Jesus brings a wonderful hope for the present and also for the future in an uncertain world.

The gospel gave Donald Cargill a wonderful hope in the face of impending death. Cargill was a Scottish Christian who was martyred for his faith in Jesus. He was condemned by the government and sentenced to the gallows. When he went to the scaffold for his execution, Cargill said these moving words, although it was said that the drums were beaten in an attempt to drown out his voice:

> Now I am near to getting to my crown, which shall be sure; for I bless the Lord, and desire all of you to bless him that he hath brought me here, and makes me triumph over devils, and men, and sin – they shall wound me no more. I forgive all men the wrongs they have done to me, and pray the Lord may forgive all the wrongs that any of the elect have done against him. I pray that sufferers may be kept from sin, and helped to know their duty – reading and preaching, praying and believing, wanderings, re-proaches, and sufferings. Welcome joy unspeakable and full of glory.

Jesus

'*Remember Jesus Christ, raised from the dead, descended from David. This is my gospel, for which I am suffering even to the point of being chained like a criminal. But God's word is not chained*' (2 Timothy 2:8–9). Paul's suffering was worth it. He was prepared to suffer anything so he could spread the gospel – the glorious message of Jesus.

It was the sixteenth-century church leader, Martin Luther, who said, '*The gospel is not that which is written in books and letters, but rather a spoken message and a living word – a voice which sounds out into the world and is publicly proclaimed that it might be heard everywhere.*' Precise definitions are sometimes difficult, but the actual heart of the gospel – the Greek word *kerygma* – is found throughout the New Testament, but a different emphasis is put on it each time, with bits added or taken away depending on the situation, and on who was communicating with whom. One verse, probably the most famous verse in the Bible, sums it all up: '*For God so loved the world that he gave his one and only Son, that whoever believes in him shall not perish but have eternal life*' (John 3:16).

That one verse is the gospel in a nutshell. We are so special to God that he sent his one and only Son, knowing full well that he would suffer and die so that we could know him. Many Jews wrongly believed the Messiah was coming just for them, to their nation. But Jesus tells us that he came for the whole world, Jews and Gentiles alike, so everyone who believes in him won't die but instead will live for ever. Now that's what I call good news.

Hospitality

Above all, love each other deeply, because love covers over a multitude of sins. Offer hospitality to one another without grumbling. Each one should use whatever gift he has received to serve others, faithfully administering God's grace in its various forms. If anyone speaks, he should do it as one speaking the very words of God. If anyone serves, he should do it with the strength God provides, so that in all things God may be praised through Jesus Christ. (1 Peter 4:8–11)

A very wealthy, religious, little old lady was a soft touch for any down-and-out she happened to meet on the street. One day she met a very shabbily dressed man who was wandering down the road where she lived, and impulsively pressed a five pound note into his hand, smiled warmly and whispered, 'God speed' as he went on his way. The next day the tramp knocked at the door of her house and said, 'Here's your hundred pounds. Godspeed came in first and paid twenty to one.'

Being generous and hospitable is something we can all do and it can make a tremendous impact on those we know. *'Hospitality is one form of worship'*, says the ancient Jewish proverb, and as such it is a key tool in our evangelism toolkit. So why, I wonder, do we often feel we need to try the hardest evangelistic things first – like handing out tracts or knocking on doors, which can be pretty soul-destroying after a few setbacks.

We've seen already that over three-quarters of people come

to faith in Jesus through friendships and relationships, so inviting friends and neighbours over for a meal, for example, is fun and enjoyable, and can also have a great impact on our non-believing guests. There is a Danish proverb that says: '*When there is room in the heart there is room in the house.*'

When your friends come to your house, they can see you share the same problems as they do, that you are normal, yet different, because Jesus lives in you and has changed your priorities and motives in life. You shouldn't need to grow a beard or hit people over the head with a tambourine while singing 'Lord of the dance' for your friends to see there's something different about you. The New Testament talks an awful lot about hospitality and I particularly love the story of Matthew the tax collector, whom Jesus had chosen to be a disciple.

> As Jesus went on from there, he saw a man named Matthew sitting at the tax collector's booth. 'Follow me,' he told him, and Matthew got up and followed him. While Jesus was having dinner at Matthew's house, many tax collectors and 'sinners' came and ate with him and his disciples. (Matthew 9:9–10)

In those days, tax collectors were classed together with robbers and even murderers, yet Jesus chose Matthew to be one of his closest friends and co-workers. This would have been a huge sacrifice for Matthew, as he would have been very wealthy, indeed probably the richest of all the disciples. In spite of this, he abandoned his job and invited his friends and business colleagues round to his house for a slap-up meal, so they too could meet Jesus.

There are many different ways that we can exercise hospitality and I'm going to mention some very practical ideas that you can use personally but also corporately. By corporate I mean things your church can do to be more welcoming and make a bigger impact on those who don't yet know Jesus.

Personal

Let's begin in the home. Meals are a great start. Everyone has to eat, and it's a great way for building friendships and relaxing together. In this sort of environment it is so easy to chat about anything and everything – including what matters to you – without fear of embarrassment or awkwardness.

If Jemma, my wife, and I are putting on a meal at home, we like to get a mix of Christians and non-Christians. Do think about this though, otherwise you could be in for an explosive evening! Bringing together guests with similar personalities, interests and occupations are a few factors that should be worth thinking through, so that conversation flows well. You may need to pre-warn your Christian friends that the evening is fun and low-key, and not an opportunity to beat your heathen friends over the head with a big black Bible or sit in a circle after the meal, singing Christian folk-songs! Instead, the evening is a chance to have a laugh and make friends.

Consider what you're going to eat. I would suggest something simple, as you the cook don't really want to be getting stressed out in the kitchen all evening; you want to be with your guests enjoying yourself. Though having said that, do put a real effort into what you're going to be serving. Obviously ask in advance if there's any food they don't really like, and whether they have any special dietary needs. I like the idea of themed nights. When I returned from a wonderful ministry time to Mexico, we had . . . yes, you guessed it, a Mexican evening. We enjoyed nachos, tacos, good quality Mexican wine and a glass of Tequila to finish. It also gave me a very natural opportunity to share what God had done on that trip.

Be creative with meals and do the best you can. Be it a buffet meal, cheese and wine evening, Pimms and pancakes, beer and curry, or an Independence Day barbecue with fireworks thrown in as well (though not literally you understand!), then make it the very best you can. And by the way, the *very best* doesn't mean the *most expensive*. Very occasionally I get taken out to very nice expensive restaurants. Of course that's a great treat, though if I'm really honest I'd probably enjoy a nice cottage pie and a pint of beer with my best friends. You don't have to spend wads of cash to be hospitable. Food and drink served with love, thought and attention get my vote every time. In fact if you did serve up a five-course *cordon bleu* meal, your friends and neighbours could feel awkward if they felt they weren't able to reciprocate your hospitality when it was your turn to go to their house.

If you're not a great chef, get a take-away in, or make the selection when your guests arrive. Personally, if we choose to do that, we'll phone the order through and then I and the other lads will go and collect the food – via the pub. This is always fun, and gives the lads a chance to chat while our wives do the same back at the house.

Perhaps it would be difficult to invite friends to your home. Maybe you're a young person who lives at home with family who aren't Christians, or maybe other factors would make entertaining at home difficult. Sorry, you're not let off the hook either – go out for the night. Book a restaurant, make up a picnic or meet at the local chippie. It's dead easy and very enjoyable.

In terms of drink, it's your call, obviously. I can think of some Christian friends I know who might be offended if we have alcohol at a dinner party, but on the other hand I can't think of any of my non-Christian friends who would feel the same. In fact, they'd probably be really surprised if there wasn't some nice wine or cans of beer in the fridge. So once again, for me, I'd rather offend my Christian friends than my non-Christian mates! But alcohol or no alcohol is maybe something you need to think about in your planning.

Corporate

As part of the body of Christ, I am sometimes ashamed by the welcome and hospitality, or rather lack of it, we show to un-believers and other guests. Here are a few ideas that will hopefully make your church and its meetings more welcoming.

Welcome team

- The welcome team needs to be made up of friendly people (sounds obvious I know but don't put miseries on the door) who smile, shake hands, introduce themselves and welcome people as they come through the door to your meeting.
- The welcomer should proactively then introduce the newcomer to someone else from the church who they can sit with.
- They then invite the newcomer out for a coffee or back to lunch, or try to make an appointment to see them in the week.

Welcome packs

- As part of the meeting, the leader or vicar should welcome guests. I wouldn't personally recommend asking them to stand and shout their name and where they're from as this can be embarrassing. Maybe ask them to raise a hand, so they can be given a free gift.
- This free gift is of course one of your welcome packs, which should contain the following at the very bare minimum:

  1 A good-quality, easy-to-read book about Christianity
  2 A modern translation Bible or New Testament or at the very least a Gospel
  3 A sheet or programme with details of church meetings for all ages
  4 Colouring sheet(s) and a pack of crayons for children
  5 Contact details
  6 A response form.

- Consider putting together four different welcome packs that basically contain the above but are geared for different age groups.

  1 Tinies: for the under 5s
  2 Children: aged 5–10
  3 Young people: 11–16
  4 Adults.

The meeting itself

1 Welcome guests and explain what's going to be happening in the meeting.
2 Explain what's going on from the front.
3 Be seeker-sensitive.
4 Introduce by name the worship leader, speaker, etc.
5 Ditch all religious jargon. 'Blessed', 'saved', 'washed in the blood' are most definitely out!
6 Give an opportunity for response.
7 Expect, if they are present, unbelievers to get saved.
8 Remember the words of the apostle Paul, writing to the church in Colosse, '*Be wise in the way you act towards outsiders; make the most of every opportunity*' (Colossians 4:5).

Refreshments afterwards

I caused a bit of a stir in our church when I suggested we could improve our hospitality after our Sunday meetings. I do get very annoyed by burning my hand while having a cup of coffee in a plastic cup after church each week. I suggested getting proper cups and you'd have thought I'd suggested denying the virgin birth for the uproar it caused! Seriously though, you need to think about:

- Investing in proper cups for hot drinks. If this is simply not possible – like our church you might not have your own building with storage facilities – consider purchasing plastic cup-holders.
- Serving decent coffee and tea – maybe even from a proper cafetiere.
- Ditching the awful long-life milk and use real, proper milk or even cream in coffee.
- Having nice, bright, colourful beakers for cold drinks for the children.
- Serving home-made cakes, doughnuts or even Danish pastries instead of the cheapest biscuits money can buy.

I'm sure stingy readers, having got this far, will be shaking their heads and tutting away at the expense and inconvenience of my suggestions. Well, so what! Of course no one in their right mind would look forward to washing up 200 cups and saucers every Sunday after church, and it's perfectly obvious that the thought of simply throwing away cheap plastic cups wins every time. But these things do matter. Our God is a generous God. He showed his great love and generosity for us by sending his most precious Son into the world. That's what God is like. I reckon we can make a tremendous impact on our friends if we try to be a little more like that. Let me finish with a quote from one of the most celebrated writers of the seventeenth century, and author of *The Pilgrim's Progress*, John Bunyan, '*A man there was, and they called him mad; the more he gave, the more he had.*' It says it all.

Imaginative Evangelism

I'm going to be throwing out loads of ideas in this chapter, most of which I have tried in one form or the other. It's so important to be up-to-date and creative with all our evangelistic endeavours. Albert Einstein said: '*Imagination is more important than knowledge*' so that's something to seriously think about.

I guess whatever you're organising in an evangelistic context in terms of gospel content would probably fall into one of the following categories which I have distinguished by colours of traffic lights: red, amber and green.

Red

This would be the sort of event that will integrate Christians with your unbelieving friends without any fears of Bible-bashing or hard sell. Often a major hurdle to cross in our evangelism is the smashing of misconceptions that non-Christians have about the Church and Christians. *Red* events would probably contain no gospel content at all, from the front anyway. They are simply events for fun and fellowship, that are put on by Christians to be good news to the community.

Amber

Amber events will be fun, but will also contain appropriate, low-key gospel content. I organise meal-based events for the church that I'm part of, with well-known celebrities who also have a story to tell of how they met Jesus. We hold them at a local pub, include a three-course carvery meal, and after the dinner our special guest will share their story for around forty-five minutes or so. These are always tremendous events, and we actually find that non-Christians are inviting their own unbelieving friends to these events, doing the hard work for us. An appeal for salvation is not appropriate at *amber* events, though we always have a supply of free evangelistic books for those who want to know more. At the events that we run, it's really not unusual for over two-thirds of the audience to be guests.

Green

This is the green light for you to make an appeal for salvation. *Green* events will come later down the line as you build up trust and friendships with your contacts. Have an evangelist give a clear appeal for salvation and expect people to become Christians.

It's important to carefully think through your evangelistic strategy and plan a combination of *red*, *amber* and *green* events that your church can buy into and feel comfortable inviting their friends to. Virtually any of the following could fit into any of the three categories. So, here follows a load of ideas to get you thinking creatively.

Events

- Concert – band, solo artist, string quartet
- Cabaret – with music, drama and comedy
- Chat shows – use this as a fun way of hearing testimonies from local or nationally known Christians, who can confidently share their story of meeting God
- Theme nights – I recently organised a 1960s night, with disco, bar, buffet and a cabaret spot from John Gaughan, who sang with Herman's Hermits in the 1960s. John performed and shared his amazing story. Alternatively, get your afro wigs and flares out for a 1970s night and hire an Abba tribute band.
- Barn dance

- Barbecue
- Line dancing
- Quiz night
- Movie night – get a big-screen TV or video projector and watch a movie together. Don't forget popcorn and hot dogs though, and please don't feel you need to show *Jesus of Nazareth*, *Ben Hur* or indeed any Christian films!
- Pantomime – great fun around Christmas.

Sports

As well as cricket and netball teams, my own church has had a darts team in our local pub league for over fifteen years. I spoke to our captain, Mark 'Jocky' Wilson, who explained that the aim in the early days was to evangelise the whole league within two years. Realistically that didn't happen as such, but the team raised the profile of the church in a very short space of time. They've also shown that Christians can have a laugh, and have been able to have some great conversations about what they believe. Also, two people have become Christians through the team. Both men were playing for the church team at the time, though Monday-night darts was the nearest thing to church they attended on a regular basis. Through friendships and relationships they became Christians.

I think it would be fantastic to have church teams involved in all sports – not setting up 'Christian' leagues – but by being good news and mixing a bit of salt and light around in normal 'secular' leagues. Here are another ten sports activities you could get involved with, although I realise there are many, many more that I haven't mentioned.

1 Pool
2 Snooker
3 Tenpin bowling
4 Squash
5 Golf – believe it or not, there is an American website for Christian golfers, whose aim it is to convert fellow golfers to

Christ. It even uses the acronym GOLFER – God Offers Love Forgiveness Eternal Redemption. How about that?!

6 Football
7 Swimming
8 Fishing
9 Tennis
10 Basketball.

Food for thought

There's something wonderful about sitting down and eating and drinking together. I organised a football night recently, where we enjoyed a meal together at a pub, followed by an after-dinner talk by Alan Mullery MBE, the former Spurs and England international footballer and SKY soccer pundit. Alan shared his Christian faith, peppered with lots of footballing anecdotes. To quote my non-Christian neighbour Chris, who I'd invited along: 'Steve, that was the best 'f★★★★★g' night I've been to in years.' What a great compliment!

Once again there are loads of different ways of eating and fellowshipping together, with or without a speaker:

- Coffee mornings
- Cheese and wine
- Wine-tasting evening
- Pimms and pancakes
- Beer and skittles
- Barbecues
- Breakfast
- Lunch
- Dinner
- Theme nights – Mexican, Spanish, Chinese, American . . . If your church has missionaries, evangelists or other workers working abroad, it could be appropriate to focus on their work as well as enjoying the food and drink.

Outdoors

- Door to door
- Street surveys
- Gardening – offer to help out elderly neighbours with basic gardening.
- Streetwork – a fantastic way to reach hundreds with the gospel – lots more about this later.
- Windscreen-washing – I've done this to great effect all over the country. You offer a free windscreen wash and at the end of the clean, give a tract or an invite to an evangelistic event.
- Shoe-shining – similar to windscreen-washing in its aim.
- Street carnival – organise stalls, refreshments, music and entertainment
- Fun day – similar to the above, though you could hold this outside your church's premises on a hot, summer's day.
- Fishing trip
- Treasure hunt – finish with a picnic and games, or at a pub if it's adults only.

In the news

- Newspapers – contact the editor of your local newspaper and offer to write a Christian comment column on a regular basis. My own local newspaper, the *Littlehampton Gazette*, has a monthly page with information from the churches in our area, made up of news and views and what's on.
- Magazines – my friend Paul Sinclair is a motorbike enthusiast as well as being an Elim minister. Paul writes a regular Christian column for national motorbike magazines, where through biking experiences he shares the gospel with thousands of bikers.

Church meetings

People are obviously expecting to hear more of the gospel at these meetings but don't forget to make these really good, seeker-sensitive events:

- Christenings and dedications – annual baptisms in 1998 numbered 177,000, and according to the *Daily Telegraph*, 25 million people living in England today have been baptised by the Church of England. That's nearly half of the entire population.
- Healing meetings – raise people's faith and expect God to show up.
- Special Sunday guest services
- Christmas carol service
- Easter special
- Mothers' and Fathers' Days
- Pentecost Sunday.

Away days

- Activity weekends – go away for an entire weekend together for a whole host of exciting outdoor activities.
- Days out – take the lads away on a jolly boys' beano to Margate, or wherever for the day, for some good male bonding.
- Day trip to France.
- Golf tournament – finishing with a meal and presentation of awards.
- Night out – go to the theatre, the opera, a concert – classic or rock, or see a football match together.

Family

If you have a young family then get involved with the following:

- Parent and toddler groups
- Playgroups
- Pre-schools
- Nursery schools
- Schools.

Help out in whatever way you can; offer support, personnel and other help when needed. Help with fund-raising and become a member of the parent-teacher association. If you have the time and inclination you might feel you'd be a good school governor. You're not there to preach, you're there to be good news. Offer practical help, perhaps as a classroom assistant; take an assembly; or bring in other members of your church to help out at specific points during the year.

Courses

I'm sure you have a lot of untapped talent in your church. How about scrapping your midweek meeting or house-group for a term, and instead encouraging every member to choose and attend a course, run by other people from your church? They would be great things to invite guests to. Here are twenty ideas off the top of my head:

 1 *Alpha*
 2 Bible studies
 3 Car maintenance
 4 Cookery
 5 Wine-making
 6 DIY
 7 Interior design
 8 Languages
 9 Sports coaching
10 Dance
11 Drama
12 Journalism
13 Creative writing
14 Music lessons
15 Model-making
16 First-aid
17 Photography
18 Painting
19 Theology
20 Parentcraft.

In closing this chapter, let me tell you about the Gate Church in Dundee. They found traditional outreach methods didn't really work very well, so they turned to more creative ways of reaching the lost. Their evangelistic programmes now include a 'Student Feed' where they distribute free lunches to 350 students each week. They attract 2,000 skateboarders, in-line skaters and BMX bikers to 'The Factory', and their pre-school day nursery is regularly commended by the local authorities. Some have come to faith through these initiatives and they are winning their city's attention. Stuart Brunton, the main leader, admitted, 'We're no longer that hidden little church. We're quite visible now.'

I-M

Jesus

He was born in an obscure village, the child of a peasant woman. He grew up in yet another village, where he worked in a carpenter's shop until he was thirty. Then for three years he was an itinerant preacher.

He never wrote a book. He never held an office. He never had a family or owned a big house. He didn't go to college. He never travelled more than 200 miles from the place where he was born. He did none of the things one usually associates with greatness. He had no credentials but himself.

He was only thirty-three when the tide of public opinion turned against him. His friends ran away. He was nailed to a cross between two thieves. While he was dying, his executioners gambled for his clothing, the only property he had on earth.

Twenty centuries have come and gone and today he is the central figure of the human race. All the armies that ever marched, all the navies that ever sailed, all the parliaments that have ever sat, all the kings that ever reigned, put together, have not affected the life of man on this earth as that one solitary life.

Very simply, we do evangelism because of Jesus, the most extraordinary person ever to have walked the face of the earth. He's changed our lives for the better and we want others to know about his wonderful love, forgiveness, acceptance and promise of new life too.

I'd like to take the opportunity in this chapter to remind ourselves afresh of just ten things that made Jesus so unique.

He kept company with outcasts

One of the numerous problems the religious establishment had with Jesus was the company he kept. In fact one of his best friends was a prostitute! One day they asked his followers, '*Why does your teacher eat with tax collectors and sinners?*' It's no exaggeration to say that murderers, robbers and tax collectors would be classed together; yet Jesus chose Matthew the tax collector to be a disciple, and consequently one of his closest twelve friends and indeed confidant.

Jesus' answer was clear and unequivocal, '*It is not the healthy people who need a doctor, but the sick.*' He went on, '*I did not come to invite good people but to invite sinners.*' And that includes us all. We might not have ever murdered someone or robbed a bank, but I know if we're honest we've all thought, said or done things that are wrong. I'm afraid that makes us all 'sinners', whether we like it or not.

He claimed to be God

In 1936, a radio broadcast was to be transmitted to America from England. Just before the voice of King Edward VIII was to be heard, someone tripped over a wire in the control room at the radio station and snapped the only line of communication between the two countries. The engineers were frantic. With only a few moments remaining before airtime, a quick-thinking apprentice grasped the two broken ends of the wire and bridged the gap. Seconds later the king's address was broadcast to America. In a very real sense, his words were being transmitted through the body of that man.

That's a picture of the essence of Christianity. Jesus was quite literally, God in a body. He came to experience every emotion that we feel: laughter, hope, pain, despair. God, in the person of Jesus, entered our time-space world to experience it first-hand for himself and to make a real difference.

He revived the dead

On three different occasions Jesus brought people back from the dead. One day in a small town called Nain, some ten miles southeast of Nazareth, Jesus stood and watched a funeral procession. It was a heartbreaking sight − a devastated widow, her husband already deceased and now her only son dead too. The coffin, unlike our modern coffins, was probably just a board on which the body lay. The funeral cortège passed by and Jesus stopped it. He told the boy's mother to stop crying, and told the corpse to get up. The young man sat up immediately and began to talk.

And this happened on more than one occasion. Hardly the image of a boring religious hippie in a flowing white dress, is it?! These recorded miracles are only just scratching the surface, though. It's interesting that in total only fifty or so days of Jesus' work is touched upon in all the combined Gospels. That's not a lot in three years of public travelling or, put another way, in just over 1,000 days. My calculator tells me that means just under 5 per cent of the days that Jesus was ministering are actually recorded. Just imagine all the conversations, the fun and normality, and indeed all the other miraculous things that we never even heard about. It's hardly any wonder that John wrote, '*Jesus did many other things as well. If every one of them were written down, I suppose that even the whole world would not have room for the books that would be written*' (John 21:25).

He turned water into wine

Being an interesting sort of person, Jesus often got invited to parties. On one occasion he was at a wedding reception with his family and friends when quite unexpectedly the organisers ran out of wine. Unlike our short weddings today with the service over in an hour, and then a two-hour reception, in Jesus' day it was quite a bit more than a sausage roll, a mushroom vol-au-vent and a slice of cake! Weddings then usually took about a week. On the first day, the couple exchanged vows under a canopy, then for the next six days or more, the happy couple and all the guests celebrated with dancing, games, music, food and wine.

It sounds quite a party, doesn't it? And it was, until they ran out of wine! It was a disaster, to say the least. The Bible tells us Jesus went and found six jars of water, each holding around 100 litres and he miraculously turned the contents into the very best wine, over 900 bottles' worth. Dare I suggest that since that day in Cana, some 2,000 years ago, certain aspects of the Church have been trying to turn it back to water again!

He was considered a failure

I suppose by current standards of success, Jesus might have been considered a failure. He wasn't popular, or even well-liked. Indeed after one of his sermons, all his followers deserted him, except for the twelve disciples. He was a political failure too, and all levels of government first rejected him, before they conspired to kill him.

He wasn't particularly good-looking, and didn't have a beautiful wife, or string of glamorous girlfriends. He had no money or possessions, no offices, not even a house. In fact most of the time he lived rough. He didn't even have many friends, and those he did have often hurt him, eventually abandoned him, and one even betrayed him to death. Yet despite his apparent failure by these standards, Jesus has changed the lives of billions of men and women, boys and girls across the centuries.

He offered forgiveness to everyone

In the New Testament, the Greek word most often used for 'forgiveness' actually means 'sending away' or 'release'. Literally it's the taking away of wrongdoing and the guilt that goes with it. Jesus once told a story of a wayward son who rebelled against his father (Luke 15 – the Prodigal Son), but who was received back with open arms and forgiveness.

I'm sure we all know from personal experience that forgiveness isn't always an easy thing, and in many ways it has a real cost to it. Christians believe that through Jesus' death and resurrection he made God's forgiveness possible for our wrong thoughts, words and actions. In other words, God's forgiveness cost God the life of his one and only Son.

He fell out with religious people

Religious people could never figure Jesus out. He started his public ministry at the age of thirty and his radical words and action took him across the country. After three incredible years he had made many friends, but many enemies too – mainly of the religious variety – and they schemed and plotted to kill him.

This was because Jesus spoke out against religion and its endless rules and regulations and instead talked about 'life', abundant life, through knowing God. This new life was for everyone, Jew and Gentile. Jesus was a breath of fresh air and upset the status quo of the old religious establishment who decided to get rid of him. In April, around the year AD 30, they plotted against him. While Jesus was in a town called Bethany, the Jewish court – the Sanhedrin – were meeting in the high priest's palace to arrange for his arrest and execution. His life was about to come to an end.

He was killed for speaking the truth

Jesus was brutally murdered for telling the truth. The truth was that he was the Son of God who came to bring everlasting life. His natural earthly life lasted only thirty-three years before he was crucified – the cruellest and the most painful death that has ever been invented.

The moment he died the sun went dark and a curtain was torn in the Temple. The darkening sky was a supernatural occurrence and was a sign to the Romans and the other non-Jews. The tearing of the curtain had a great deal of religious significance for the Jews, as the curtain represented separation between God and humankind, and now it was destroyed – indeed it was torn from top to bottom. Access to God was made available through Jesus and was now the right of anyone, Jew and non-Jew alike.

An anonymous author once made this striking comparison:

Socrates taught for forty years, Plato for fifty, Aristotle for forty, and Jesus for only three. Yet the influence of Christ's three-year ministry infinitely transcends the impact left by the combined 130 years of teaching from these men who were among the greatest philosophers of all antiquity. Jesus painted no pictures; yet some of the finest paintings of Raphael, Michelangelo and Leonardo de Vinci received their inspiration from him. Jesus wrote no poetry; but Dante, Milton and scores of the world's greatest poets were inspired by him. Jesus composed no music; still Haydn, Handel, Beethoven, Bach and Mendelssohn reached their highest perfection of melody in the hymns, symphonies and oratorios they composed in his praise. Every sphere of human greatness has been enriched by this humble Carpenter from Nazareth.

He came back from the dead

On the Friday Jesus was dead, there was no doubt about it. He had been brutally crucified, then a Roman soldier stuck his spear into his side, to make sure he was dead. Blood and water poured out from his heart. His body was peeled off the cross and placed in a tomb, and the grave was then guarded.

On that first Easter Sunday, the women who approached the tomb couldn't fail to notice that the massive stone covering it had been moved and the body was gone. This was quite extraordinary.

The women were puzzled by the scene before them, when suddenly two men in bright shining clothes appeared. Absolutely terrified, the women fell to the floor as the men said to them, '*Why are you looking among the dead for one who is alive? He is not here; he has been raised.*' As they were leaving, one of the women, Mary Magdalene, then saw Jesus for herself. At the time she didn't properly recognise him; instead she thought it the caretaker, doing odd jobs around the cemetery. It was of course Jesus, who later appeared to his disciples and hundreds of others for a period of forty days, before he went back to heaven. He was alive again.

He offered people a new start

Jesus once said, '*I am the light of the world. Whoever follows me will never walk in darkness but will have the light of life*' (John 8:12). Not endless rules and regulations or boring religion. Instead Jesus offers new life, hope and meaning, a destiny and a reason for living.

No one can stay neutral when it comes to Jesus; we all have to make a decision. Sitting on the fence gets a bit uncomfortable, and if you spend all your life walking down the middle of the road, you're going to get hit one day. Jesus himself said this, '*He who is not with me is against me*' (Matthew 12:30).

The American evangelist, Billy Graham, told a story about Auguste Comte, the French philosopher, and Thomas Carlyle, the Scottish writer. Comte decided he was going to start a new religion that would take the place of Christianity. 'Very good, Mr Comte,' Carlyle replied, 'all you need to do will be to speak like a man never spoke before, to live like no other man ever lived. Then be crucified, and rise again on the third day, and get the world to believe that you are still alive. Then your religion will have a chance to get on.'

Christianity is no dead religion; it's alive, because its founder Jesus is still alive. Pilgrims still travel to Israel to visit the tomb he was buried in, but there is no coffin or body. Jesus is alive, and he wants a personal friendship with people. And how can they hear if we don't tell them? That's why we do evangelism, so let's get on with the job.

I-M

Knowing What to Say

Many years ago a young man joined a monastery in which the monks were allowed to speak only two words every seven years. After the first seven years had passed the new monk met with the abbot who asked him, 'Well, what are your two words?' 'Food's bad,' replied the man, who then went back to spend another seven years of silence before once again meeting with the abbot. 'What are your two words now?' asked the clergyman. 'Bed's hard,' responded the man. Seven years later – twenty-one years after his initial entry into the monastery – the man met with the abbot for the third and final time.

'And what are your two words this time?' he was asked.

'I quit.'

'Well, I'm not surprised,' answered the disgusted abbot, 'all you've done since you got here is complain.'

Our words and the way we communicate them matter, particularly if we only have a short time to share our message, where every word counts. In the New Testament a man called Nicodemus came to Jesus once with a stack of questions. He was an important Jewish ruler and teacher and he had many questions to ask.

> Now there was a man of the Pharisees named Nicodemus, a member of the Jewish ruling council. He came to Jesus at night and said, 'Rabbi, we know you are a teacher who has come from God. For no-one could perform the miraculous signs you are doing if God were not with him.'

In reply Jesus declared, 'I tell you the truth, no-one can see the kingdom of God unless he is born again.'

'How can a man be born when he is old?' Nicodemus asked. 'Surely he cannot enter a second time into his mother's womb to be born!'

Jesus answered, 'I tell you the truth, no-one can enter the kingdom of God unless he is born of water and the Spirit. Flesh gives birth to flesh, but the Spirit gives birth to spirit. You should not be surprised at my saying, "You must be born again." The wind blows wherever it pleases. You hear its sound, but you cannot tell where it comes from or where it is going. So it is with everyone born of the Spirit.'

'How can this be?' Nicodemus asked.

'You are Israel's teacher,' said Jesus, 'and do you not understand these things? I tell you the truth, we speak of what we know, and we testify to what we have seen, but still you people do not accept our testimony. I have spoken to you of earthly things and you do not believe; how then will you believe if I speak of heavenly things? No-one has ever gone into heaven except the one who came from heaven – the Son of Man. Just as Moses lifted up the snake in the desert, so the Son of Man must be lifted up, that everyone who believes in him may have eternal life.' (John 3:1–15)

You'll notice how, in his dealings with Nicodemus, Jesus refused to lose his focus and be sidetracked. Instead he got straight to what he wanted to say, using language and illustrations that Nicodemus would understand. In our conversations we need to do the same. It's so important to stay focused and clear about what we want to say. Of course it's unlikely you'll ever have the time to go through the entire Bible while witnessing on the streets one Saturday afternoon, so it's helpful to select the important facts that people need to know and understand if they want to become a Christian.

What follows isn't a magical formula. At the end of the day, people are people, not scalps or statistics, and our communication of the gospel will of course differ depending on whom we are talking with. I've pondered over the chapter long and hard as the gospel isn't really about a technique, principles or concepts – not even 'four spiritual laws'. It's about Jesus and whether we chose to walk with him. Having said that, when I present the gospel, I often use the following framework as a guide, using four key points – God, Sin, Jesus and Faith – which I allow God to breathe through. It's always helpful to back up what we're saying with verses from the Bible alongside some illustrations that people can relate to.

God

In the beginning God planned a great relationship with people.

Scriptures

So God created human beings in his own image. (Genesis 1:27, NIVI)

The LORD, the LORD, the compassionate and gracious God, slow to anger, abounding in love and faithfulness, maintaining love to thousands, and forgiving wickedness, rebellion and sin. (Exodus 34:6–7)

From one man he made every nation of men, that they should inhabit the whole earth; and he determined the times set for them and the exact places where they should live. God did this so that men would seek him and perhaps reach out for him and find him, though he is not far from each one of us. (Acts 17:26–7)

Illustration

A little boy was working hard on a drawing and his dad asked him what he was doing. The reply came back, 'Drawing a picture of God.'

His father said, 'Well, that must be quite hard, son. Nobody knows what God looks like.'

But the little boy was undeterred and continued to draw. He

looked at his picture with satisfaction and said very matter-of-factly, 'They will in a few minutes.'

Sin

People rebelled against God and sin separated us from God.

Scriptures

Who is a God like you, who pardons sin and forgives the transgression of the remnant of his inheritance? You do not stay angry for ever but delight to show mercy. (Micah 7:18–19)

For all have sinned and fall short of the glory of God. (Romans 3:23)

If we confess our sins, he is faithful and just and will forgive us our sins and purify us from all unrighteousness. (1 John 1:9)

Illustration

Originally the word 'sin' wasn't a spiritual word, but a sporting term used in archery that archers used to describe missing their target with their arrows. In the same way, we've all missed the target that God planned for us.

Jesus

Jesus came and died to take the punishment our sin deserves.

Scriptures

For God so loved the world that he gave his one and only Son, that whoever believes in him shall not perish but have eternal life. For God did not send his Son into the world to condemn the world, but to save the world through him. (John 3:16–17)

The thief comes only to steal and kill and destroy; I have

come that they may have life, and have it to the full. (John 10:10)

But God demonstrates his own love for us in this: While we were still sinners, Christ died for us. (Romans 5:8)

Illustration
Nikolai Berdyaev, who abandoned Marxism for Christianity, insists that neither history nor theology nor the church brought him to the Christian faith, but a simple Christian lady known only as Mother Maria. Berdyaev was present at a concentration camp when the Nazis were murdering Jews in gas chambers. One distraught mother refused to part with her baby. When Maria saw that the officer was only interested in numbers, without a word she pushed the mother aside and quickly took her place. This selfless action revealed to Berdyaev the heart of Christianity, and what Jesus achieved when he died on the cross.

Faith

We confess our sins and commit our lives to God

Scriptures
You will keep in perfect peace him whose mind is steadfast, because he trusts in you. Trust in the LORD for ever, for the LORD, the LORD, is the Rock eternal. (Isaiah 26:3–4)

That if you confess with your mouth, 'Jesus is Lord,' and believe in your heart that God raised him from the dead, you will be saved. For it is with your heart that you believe and are justified, and it is with your mouth that you confess and are saved. (Romans 10:9)

For it is by grace you have been saved, through faith – and this not from yourselves, it is the gift of God – not by works, so that no-one can boast. (Ephesians 2:8–9)

Illustration

Just imagine there was a medical breakthrough and scientists found a cure for the common cold. We all suffer with colds from time to time, and this new medicine would cure all the symptoms within five minutes. But it would only be any good if you actually tried it by taking a spoonful. As effective as the cold cure might be, its benefits would never be enjoyed unless you took it. The same is true of becoming a Christian and being forgiven. Although Jesus has provided the possibility for us through his death on the cross, what he accomplished there will do us no good unless we receive him.

Let me make the important point again before we look at another method for sharing the gospel: any communication that persuades people to come to Jesus isn't just down to us. Witnessing isn't selling double-glazing by clever techniques, neither is it brainwashing or beating folk over the head with the biggest black Bible you can find until they say 'yes'.

Of course God uses us as human communicators, which is awesome, because sharing your faith is great, but it is ultimately God who does the real work. We can explain the gospel to our friends and answer all their tough questions, we can even tell them that they have sinned, but it is the Holy Spirit that convicts them of their sin. '*When he comes, he will convict the world of guilt in regard to sin and righteousness and judgment*' (John 16:8).

We can save no one without God, but of course God can do it without us. In fact I'm told that most Muslims become Christians through God speaking to them in dreams. God doesn't have to use us, but the thing is he loves to use us. We are his co-workers in communicating his message of salvation.

So here follows another framework that you can use for communicating the good news. It's certainly not original to me; in fact it's very old and systematically takes the enquirer through the book of Romans. I often use the Roman Road if I'm witnessing abroad. Whichever country I go to, I always endeavour to purchase a Bible or at the very least a New Testament in the language of the country I'm in, and highlight the following verses. So even if you're as bad as I am at speaking foreign languages you too can share the gospel message, without even uttering one word.

The original version of the Roman Road started with 'sin', which I don't think is the most positive place to start, so I hope you don't mind that I've switched it around a bit so it starts with God's creative love.

The Roman Road

For since the creation of the world God's invisible qualities – his eternal power and divine nature – have been clearly seen, being understood from what has been made, so that men are without excuse. (Romans 1:20)

For all have sinned and fall short of the glory of God. (Romans 3:23)

For the wages of sin is death, but the gift of God is eternal life in Christ Jesus our Lord. (Romans 6:23)

Therefore, there is now no condemnation for those who are in Christ Jesus, because through Christ Jesus the law of the Spirit of life set me free from the law of sin and death. (Romans 8:1–2)

That if you confess with your mouth, 'Jesus is Lord,' and believe in your heart that God raised him from the dead, you will be saved. (Romans 10:9)

Therefore, I urge you, brothers, in view of God's mercy, to offer your bodies as living sacrifices, holy and pleasing to God – this is your spiritual act of worship. Do not conform any longer to the pattern of this world, but be transformed by the renewing of your mind. Then you will be able to test and approve what God's will is – his good, pleasing and perfect will. (Romans 12:1–2)

I hope you agree what a good method it is. Don't be put off by the fact that you've got a memory like a sieve, and will never remember all six verses. Help is at hand. Why not just commit the first verse, Romans 1:20, to memory, and then in the margin of your Bible next to that verse, have the next reference – Romans 3:23 – written down and so on. That will make life an awful lot easier.

I-M

Leading Someone to Christ

It was an interesting situation. Jeff started to go out with Suzy whom he had met at college. The problem was that Suzy was a Christian but Jeff wasn't. Now Jeff was a smashing lad, but we knew, and Suzy knew, that the situation wasn't ideal. After a short time, Jeff started to go to church and understandably, we were all very excited. But although Jeff seemed to enjoy the meetings and became friends with loads of Christians he didn't become a believer himself.

So, some six months down the line, I asked him if he wanted to come with me to Brunel University where the Christian Union had invited me to speak at an evangelistic event in the student union bar. Jeff agreed to come along and keep me company. At the end of my talk I returned to where we were sitting and asked Jeff what he thought.

'It was great, mate,' he replied.

'And the stuff about God?' I asked.

'Yeah, that made a lot of sense too.'

I seemed to be on a roll here, so I bit the bullet and asked the big question. 'Well, why don't you become a Christian then?'

'I'd love to,' was his unexpected reply.

I almost fell off my bar stool, but recovered quickly enough to have the privilege of leading Jeff to the Lord, then and there. Now, I'm nothing special – I just asked the question. In fact I reckon Jeff might have become a Christian months earlier if someone else had asked him.

The fact of the matter is, sooner or later, if you keep on

witnessing and taking risks by stepping out in faith, you will be leading people to the Lord on a consistent basis too. Making the big introduction is one of the most wonderful things you can do, but is a step that many Christians are scared to take.

Imagine this unlikely scenario: a salesman in a large high-street electrical store shows you a brand new television. It's the latest thing on the market, 40-inch screen with Dolby surround sound, remote control and with an integrated DVD. It's available in any colour you like, they deliver it free, and is available on interest-free credit – you can even buy now and pay in five years' time! You agree it would be just perfect for you, when the salesman suddenly says goodbye, manhandles you out of the shop and closes the door. You're left there, standing outside the store, scratching your head and thinking to yourself, 'I want it, but how do I get it?'

I hope you forgive the daft analogy, but I have found something like it is often the case with our witnessing. We sometimes tend to forget that the gospel works, and people are often ready to respond to what we've shared with them. But we often don't – be it through embarrassment or fear of rejection or whatever – give them the chance. Of course sometimes they might say 'no', but many times they will say 'yes' and you will introduce them to Jesus.

If they do say 'no' then that's their prerogative. Do make sure they've understood what you've said, but don't push it. At the end of the day it's their decision and we shouldn't bully anyone into the kingdom of God. In the New Testament the rich young ruler looked ready to make a commitment, but decided he wasn't prepared to follow Jesus and he didn't push it. If Jesus respected people's individual freedom then we should too.

It might be that it's just too much for the person to think about and take in, in one go. They may need to think about it for a few days or so. Great. But do something practical that will help them to make a reasoned decision, like lending them a good book and arranging to pick it up and chat further within the next twenty-four hours. And of course if they're still not interested in becoming a Christian after all that, then don't stop being friends with them. The unsaved should never be seen as pew-fodder, or numbers to chalk up in your Bible. That's not on at all. One of my mates, Graham, I've known since we were four years old and humanly speaking he is nowhere near becoming a Christian, but he's still my mate and he always will be, whether he accepts Christ or not.

Many people will want to become a Christian though, and we need to make sure we introduce them to Jesus. Becoming a Christian should be a very natural process, so the following steps and framework once again should be seen as just a few simple stages through which God can release the Holy Spirit. It is this same Holy Spirit that convicts people of sin and their need of God: '*When he comes, he will convict the world of guilt in regard to sin and righteousness and judgment: in regard to sin, because men do not believe in me*' (John 16:8–9)

Make sure the person who wants to become a Christian understands the gospel properly and what is involved. They then need to do four things. To help you remember these four important steps, I spent a sleepless night coming up with what I hope might be an original and helpful mnemonic. For the extra spiritual among you, think of the special Jewish word, literally meaning '*daddy*', that the apostle Paul encouraged us to call God. For the rest of us, just think of the flared- white-jumpsuited, spangly, seventies Swedish supergroup – ABBA – and it might just aid your memory!

Admit

A person needs to admit that they've done wrong – that they have sinned, and this sin has separated them from God: '*For all have sinned and fall short of the glory of God*' (Romans 3:23). The Bible uses the word 'repentance' which literally means a deep sorrow about your actions and a turning away from all you know to be wrong. In fact, saying sorry and being sorry.

Believe

The person needs to believe that Jesus' death and resurrection were the ultimate sacrifice, and made it possible for us all to start a new life: '*For God so loved the world that he gave his one and only Son, that whoever believes in him shall not perish but have eternal life*' (John 3:16). Jesus paid the price for the death penalty our sins deserved.

Become

Now is the step for them to become a Christian by committing themselves to Jesus: '*Yet to all who received him, to those who believed in his name, he gave the right to become children of God*' (John 1:12). When you think about it logically, it's daft to live any other way. If God created us, he knows what's best for us and God's best is friendship with him, only available through Jesus.

Accept

The new Christian should accept the love and forgiveness of God and receive the Holy Spirit: '*If you then, though you are evil, know how to give good gifts to your children, how much more will your Father in heaven give the Holy Spirit to those who ask him!*' (Luke 11:13). The Holy Spirit gives us the power to change and get to know God.

How you actually pray the prayer of commitment is up to you. The way I like to do it is to pray a line at a time and ask the person to pray that line after me, either out loud or silently in their head. But do cover the above points. When I lead people to Christ, be it one-to-one or at a large meeting, I ask them to repeat the following prayer after me. I include it here to give you an idea of what I cover:

Dear Father God,
I am really sorry for my sins – for all the things I do, say and think that are wrong. I'm truly sorry and I choose to turn from these things.
I believe Jesus is the Son of God and he died on a cross and came back to life again so that I could know you personally.

I now want to become a Christian and follow you.
Please come into my life and fill me with your Holy Spirit,
    so as from today I can live my life for you.
Amen.

Afterwards, always ask the new Christian how they feel. They might be expecting a dramatic conversion experience, complete with flashing lights and a big booming voice from heaven. They might be confused or disappointed if it doesn't happen like that. The person might feel different, or they might not, so explain that the Christian faith is built upon belief, and not necessarily feelings all the time. Remind them of and reassure them with the words of Jesus: '*Here I am! I stand at the door and knock. If anyone hears my voice and opens the door, I will come in and eat with him, and he with me*' (Revelation 3:20).

Miracles

Some years ago there was large mission in my home-town, Bournemouth, with the well-known preacher, Ian Coffey. The mission was called 'He's Here'. It was subtitled 'A natural look at a supernatural God'. Thousands came to hear the gospel message in the main hall at the Bournemouth International Centre where Ian did a fantastic job, preaching the gospel each evening with hundreds becoming Christians in the process. But I've always wondered how different it might have been if instead of being a '*natural*' look, we might have glimpsed a '*supernatural*' look at a supernatural God. There's no doubt about it, signs and wonders have a funny way of getting people's attention.

Just before Jesus ascended into heaven, he told his disciples not to leave Jerusalem until they received the Holy Spirit. This Holy Spirit would give them the power they needed for their mission. You see, God always gives us the tools we need for the job: '*But you will receive power when the Holy Spirit comes on you; and you will be my witnesses in Jerusalem, and in all Judea and Samaria, and to the ends of the earth*' (Acts 1:8).

Remember how devastated the disciples were immediately after Jesus' death. They were terrified – they thought the whole plan had gone terribly wrong and they were part of its failure. As we've already seen, Jesus came into this situation and breathed on them and they received the Holy Spirit:

On the evening of that first day of the week, when the disciples were together, with the doors locked for fear of the Jews, Jesus came and stood among them and said, 'Peace be with you!' After he said this, he showed them his hands and side. The disciples were overjoyed when they saw the Lord. Again Jesus said, 'Peace be with you! As the Father has sent me, I am sending you.' And with that he breathed on them and said, 'Receive the Holy Spirit.' (John 20:19–22)

Now consider the change in these men just a few weeks later. Jesus had ascended into heaven and the apostles were in Jerusalem for Pentecost. Before the birth of the Church, Pentecost was a major party time for the Jews. Their festivities revolved around celebrating the wheat harvest and they ate, drank and were generally pretty merry.

It was then that the Holy Spirit came in a dramatic demonstration:

When the day of Pentecost came, they were all together in one place. Suddenly a sound like the blowing of a violent wind came from heaven and filled the whole house where they were sitting. They saw what seemed to be tongues of fire that separated and came to rest on each of them. All of them were filled with the Holy Spirit and began to speak in other tongues as the Spirit enabled them. (Acts 2:1–4)

Not surprisingly, this drew quite a crowd. The religious people who were watching the holy commotion thought that these men had drunk a little too much wine. Peter, indignant at their jibes and accusations of drunkenness, stood up, full of the Holy Spirit, and preached an awesome evangelistic sermon, and 3,000 were saved (Acts 2:14–41).

A little while later, while on their way to their daily prayer meeting at the Temple, Peter and John saw a blind man who asked them for money. Look at Peter's response:

'Silver or gold I do not have, but what I have I give you. In the name of Jesus Christ of Nazareth, walk.' Taking him by the right hand, he helped him up, and instantly the man's feet and ankles became strong. He jumped to his feet and began to walk. Then he went with them into the temple courts, walking and jumping, and praising God. (Acts 3:6–8)

This amazing miracle drew another large crowd, and the following day the Jewish rulers, elders and teachers of the law called Peter and John in to question them on what had happened. Peter, once again full of the Holy Spirit, replied:

'Rulers and elders of the people! If we are being called to account today for an act of kindness shown to a cripple and are asked how he was healed, then know this, you and all the people of Israel: It is by the name of Jesus Christ of Nazareth, whom you crucified but whom God raised from the dead, that this man stands before you healed.' (Acts 4:8–10)

This wonderful story goes on to explain that the Jewish leaders were staggered by the men's boldness and eloquence, especially as they had had no special training or education: '*When they saw the courage of Peter and John and realised that they were unschooled, ordinary men, they were astonished and they took note that these men had been with Jesus*' (Acts 4:13). I love those last few words, 'they took note that these men had been with Jesus'. God had impacted these once-frightened men with his power, and others saw for themselves that they had met with Jesus.

The Greek word for this 'power' is *dunamis*, from which we get our English word 'dynamite'. As we know, dynamite is a high explosive, and this *dunamis* is the same – it's an explosive power that shakes and changes things. The great news is that this same power is on offer for us today.

I'm reminded of the occasion when I and a small team had been working in sunny Herne Bay in Kent. As I recall, I don't think it was terribly sunny – in fact it was rather bleak – but I digress. My friend Chrissy and I wandered down to the seafront to do some detached youth work. We were having a great time chatting with a group of teenagers and gradually steering the conversation onto God and miracles when a young lad called Simon pulled his sleeve up to reveal a very badly scarred arm. 'Well, mate,' he said, 'do you reckon God can do anything about this?' Now I wasn't exactly sure if it was a question or a challenge, so I asked the rest of the lads to gather around in a circle as I asked God to heal their mate's arm. I really was full of faith, and the story would read considerably better if I said that his arm was miraculously healed – but it wasn't. The lads didn't seem too disappointed either, as they hadn't expected anything to happen in the first place, so we just carried on chatting and befriending them.

If I'm honest, I was a little disappointed as I was so sure I'd been obedient to God, but there wasn't really much more I could have done. The next evening we faithfully returned to the beach and saw the gang hanging around again. Simon saw us and started shouting, 'Oi, mate (he never did seem to remember my name) – my arm's better.' We ran over and he proudly displayed his unblemished arm for us all to see. God had healed him. As a result of this miracle, one person became a Christian that evening.

And that is just one example of many I could give you that I have seen with my own eyes. From what I read of the New Testament, I am more and more convinced that miracles, signs and wonders are for those who aren't Christians, as proof that God exists.

> And these signs will accompany those who believe: In my name they will drive out demons; they will speak in new tongues; they will pick up snakes with their hands; and when they drink deadly poison, it will not hurt them at all; they will place their hands on sick people, and they will get well. (Mark 16:17–18)

Let's look at one last example from the New Testament before I list a few ways to increase the power of your prayers when it comes to miracles. I fully realise that I'm probably preaching to the converted here, but these biblical accounts will build your faith. Our hero again this time is Peter.

As Peter travelled about the country, he went to visit the saints in Lydda. There he found a man named Aeneas, a paralytic who had been bedridden for eight years. 'Aeneas,' Peter said to him, 'Jesus Christ heals you. Get up and take care of your mat.' Immediately Aeneas got up. All those who lived in Lydda and Sharon saw him and turned to the Lord. (Acts 9:32–5)

Read that last line again. Because of that one miracle the entire population of two towns became Christians. We're talking about a major revival here.

As promised, here's a checklist that I hope will help you pray with more power so you will see the miraculous released to unbelievers.

Have faith

Know that God wants to start healing the person you are praying with: '*As you go, preach this message: "The kingdom of heaven is near." Heal the sick, raise the dead, cleanse those who have leprosy, drive out demons. Freely you have received, freely give*' (Matthew 10:7–8). I love the words that Basil King wrote in his book, *The Conquest of Fear*: '*Go at it boldly, and you'll find unexpected forces closing round you and coming to your aid.*' Isn't that terrific? Step out in faith, go at it boldly, and you'll find God closing round you and coming to help you. Believe it and expect it.

Check your motives

You shouldn't be praying to show off, neither should you feel pressurised to pray if you just don't feel it's right: '*But the man who has doubts is condemned if he eats, because his eating is not from faith; and everything that does not come from faith is sin*' (Romans 14:23).

Don't put the person under pressure

Don't insist that you pray for the person if they don't really want you to. If they're really uncomfortable with what you're doing then they probably will find it very hard to receive anything from God anyway. If the time's not right, take a raincheck and put it off until things are easier.

Relax

Be normal and don't suddenly get all super-spiritual and use a funny voice. There's no need to shout 'Jeee-sus' as loud as you can, with one hand hovering over the top of the person's head, while the other hand beats them up with a tambourine. Jesus was incredibly normal when he prayed for people, so be the same. Don't worry if the person doesn't shake or fall over! Relax and smile, and make the person feel at ease.

Listen to God

Hear what God has got to say for the person. There might be a deeper problem that their illness is just a symptom of. Ask God for 'keys' to unlock the situation. My friend and fellow evangelist Eric Delve believes that this is a vitally important step. He explained:

> When praying for your friends, from time to time God will give you a message for them. I do believe that discussing the gospel is necessary and that we will have to toss the arguments back and forth. But when we come with genuine concern and love for a friend and say, 'I hope you don't mind but I think God has given me a message for you – would you like to hear it?' they don't say 'no'. They want to hear it, and frequently that will begin a witnessing process in which many of the apologetic arguments have already been won because of a sense of a direct communication from the living God.

That makes so much sense. Why not give it a go?

Don't rush it

> They came to Bethsaida, and some people brought a blind man and begged Jesus to touch him. He took the blind man by the hand and led him outside the village. When he had spat on the man's eyes and put his hands on him, Jesus asked, 'Do you see anything?'
>
> He looked up and said, 'I see people; they look like trees walking around.'
>
> Once more Jesus put his hands on the man's eyes. Then his eyes were opened, his sight was restored, and he saw everything clearly. (Mark 8:22–5)

Even Jesus didn't always crack it the first time – with a blind man in Bethsaida it took him a couple of attempts, so persist in prayer.

Don't blame the person's lack of faith

If nothing happens then don't blame the recipient of prayer for their lack of faith. This is most definitely out – so don't ever do it. Don't even feel you need to explain why nothing happened. Remember the words of Oswald Chambers:

> The rationalist demands an explanation of everything: They say the reason I won't have anything to do with God is because I cannot define him. If I can define God, I am greater than the God I define. If I can define love and life, I am greater than they are.

Raise expectations

Share accounts from the Bible and from your own experience of how Jesus did and continues to do the miraculous: '*For the kingdom of God is not a matter of talk but of power*' (1 Corinthians 4:20). Raise their faith expectations and help them to believe, but always point them to Jesus. We can't heal anyone, but we know a man who can!

Speak with authority

When you're praying, speak with authority to the situation. That doesn't mean you need to holler at the top of your voice though. Where you're praying against sickness, for example, simply break its hold in the name of Jesus and pray in the healing power of God. Authority has nothing to do with decibels!

The personal touch

As you lay hands on someone, the Holy Spirit and blessing are imparted. Once again, don't feel you have to get all religious about it and lay hands on the person's head and shake it until they get a migraine. Instead, just touch an arm, or hold their hand. It's a lot more normal and yes, it does still work.

Let me finish this chapter by telling you about some astonishing miracles that are happening on a daily basis on the other side of the world. In South America, the New Life Christian Centre in Argentina has grown from 100 people in 1982 to around 12,000 people in May 2001. The church is heavily involved in evangelism and sees some 200 people (including many children) respond to God each week.

The children from the church regularly visit their peers at the Garraham Childrens' Hospital to pray for other child patients there. This hospital visitation has seen staggering results, including AIDS-infected babies being healed. In fact there have been so many miracles happening that the church has its own 'department of miracles' with a doctor working hard to verify the miracles of healing. Absolutely incredible – and it's having a huge impact in terms of salvation.

Networks

Congratulations, you're about halfway through the book and hopefully you're seeing that really effective evangelism is living the good news, it's being good news wherever you are. It's being Jesus to your next-door neighbour, to the paperboy, to your postman or the colleague who slaves away at the desk next to you at work. This method works and sees many men, women, boys and girls ushered into the kingdom.

Jesus' public ministry went very much hand in hand with his ministry to individuals and small groups. We've already looked at the conversation he had with Nicodemus, an influential and respected member of the Sanhedrin (John 3:1–21). On another occasion Jairus, one of the rulers of a synagogue, came to Jesus pleading for the life of his desperately sick twelve-year-old daughter. Jesus made time for him and raised his daughter from the dead. He always put others first.

Whether you think you do or not, you will almost definitely know a number of individuals who don't yet know Jesus. This large network of relationships is your mission field, and this should always be your starting point in evangelism. Dr Ray Bakke, an expert on urban evangelism, said that cities are institutions and do not, generally speaking, respond to events or programmes. To break through, he says, you have to look for networks and once you have plugged into them you can move a city.

Take the time right now to identify your network. I've included a framework below, and certainly won't feel offended if you should deface your copy of this book by writing individual names in the list. I guarantee as you complete your lists that you'll probably know more unbelievers than you thought you did.

Biological

This is your family. If you're anything like me – and I know I certainly am – you'll find reaching your family the hardest thing you do. I can easily stand up in front of huge crowds of unbelievers and share the gospel, but with my family, it's a different matter altogether. Often we feel that we just haven't been good witnesses to them in our words and actions. Then again, maybe it's because after years of unanswered prayers our faith for believing that they will get saved has taken a nosedive. Now might be the time to confess these things and start to pray afresh for the salvation of:

- Husband or wife
- Parents
- Grandparents
- Brothers and sisters
- Children
- Grandchildren
- Aunts and uncles
- Cousins
- Nephews and nieces.

Geographical

These are people we know in our immediate area that we have contact with.

- Neighbours
- Milkman
- Postman
- Paper deliverer
- Kleeneze or Betterware distributor

- Dustman
- Window-cleaner
- Tradesmen – builders, decorators, plumbers, gardeners, electricians, etc.
- Jehovah Witnesses!
- Other mums or dads from your children's school
- Newsagent
- Driving instructor
- Doctor
- Dentist
- Optician
- Chiropodist
- Chiropractor
- Accountant
- Solicitor
- Avon lady
- Door-to-door salespeople.

Work

This should be fairly obvious – these are people you spend hours with each week. If you don't work, you'll probably fall into one of the following categories:

- School
- College
- University
- Unemployment – people you know from the job centre
- Retirement.

Social and leisure

These would be your existing friends, but also others you spend time with socially – people you might know at:

- Sports club
- Dance studio
- Drama club

- Library
- Pub
- Nightclub
- Restaurants
- Café
- Night school
- Shops
- Parent-teacher association
- Political organisations
- Charitable organisations – Round Table, Rotary, Lions
- Women's Institute/Townswomen's Guild.

That really is quite a list, but I reckon there are a load more you can think of. If you start to realise you don't know many unbelievers then I would suggest you need to urgently reappraise your priorities so you are able to spend more time with those you know, who don't yet know Jesus. This might well mean not spending so much time with other Christians or on church-based activities.

Second, consider who in your network you realistically think might become a Christian in the short term. By 'short term' I mean within the next year or so. Attempt to identify a small group of, say, three that you can particularly concentrate on in your evangelistic endeavours. Once again, prayer is vital. When Billy Graham visited Great Britain for Mission England in 1984, the success of prayer triplets – three Christians meeting together to pray for three unsaved friends each – was phenomenal, with many coming to Christ before Dr Graham even arrived in the UK. If you're not already doing it, consider getting together with a couple of friends to meet on a regular basis to pray for those key individuals in your networks.

Alongside this, do something really proactive and start thinking of activities you can do together that you will enjoy. A word of caution here: don't always feel you need to turn each activity into a faith-sharing experience. The good news should shine out of you, and will rub off on your networks. Also start introducing them to other Christian friends, and in time invite them to events with more gospel content.

Finally, when they become Christians – and believe that they will – then this in turn opens up another mission field, in their network of relationships. New converts have much better opportunities than people who have been Christians for a longer period – they're guaranteed to know more unbelievers for starters, so help them to share their new found faith with infectious enthusiasm.

Open Air

There I was, minding my own business, while out shopping one Saturday afternoon. Out of the corner of my eye I noticed an earnest-looking chap shouting about the Bible. He had a line of six other 'brothers' behind him, looking equally as earnest and all clutching small black Bibles. Behind them stood the 'sisters' in their head scarves and overcoats. I stood for a while and watched and listened to the doom and gloom they were communicating. After they had finished their 'presentation', to which, I might add, no one was paying a blind bit of notice, I just had to go and say something.

I explained that I was a Christian from a local church, and that I had a little experience when it came to presenting the good news in the open air. I thought I was pretty diplomatic actually as I attempted to make some subtle suggestions in terms of presentation and how we should try to communicate fun and life in our message and the importance of understanding crowd dynamics. The preacher then asked where it talked about crowd dynamics in the 'Word'. I thought it would be a good time to inject some humour to try to diffuse the situation, and replied that of course it didn't mention crowd dynamics in the Bible, but neither did it mention Jesus going to the toilet, but he probably did!

The gentleman turned back to me, looked at my colourful Swatch wristwatch in disgust and declared in a loud voice: 'Well, you can't be a real Christian anyway wearing a watch like that.' And with that they all stormed off home. I couldn't believe it!

Certainly not very good news, and anyway what makes a Seconda more spiritual than a Swatch?!

Jesus did most of his ministry in the open air and other places where unbelieving men, women, boys and girls would gather. Remember the conversation he had with a Samaritan woman that is recorded in John 4. It's a wonderful example of Jesus going out of his way, smashing through cultural and religious barriers and outside, where everyone could see him, proclaiming the good news to a woman who was in great need.

As we look through the Bible we can see that neither Jesus nor his disciples relied solely on one-to-one evangelism. Many times they addressed larger crowds and most of the time these crowds were in the open air. On the Day of Pentecost, Peter stood up full of the Holy Spirit and 3,000 were saved in one go (Acts 2:14–41). Just imagine how long that would have taken if he'd used the one-to-one approach!

Many others over the years have used open-air preaching to great effect. In the middle of the eighteenth century, preachers like George Whitefield and John Wesley were awesome street preachers. The religious establishment banned both these men from preaching indoors so they went outside with their message, and those outside the church gathered in huge crowds to hear the gospel.

One afternoon in Bristol, Whitefield preached in the open air on Kingswood Common to a crowd of 200 coalminers who Wesley described as '*England's worst specimens of humanity*'. His audience kept coming back for more. As one person observed:

> When George lifted his voice for the fifth time, on the common before him was an audience of ten thousand. He had found a new pulpit from which no churchly authority could exclude him and an audience which no church could have assembled.

Even in his eighty-eighth year Wesley kept preaching outdoors. On 7 October 1790 he preached for the last time in the open air, under an ash tree in Winchelsea. Arranging the meeting for noon, so everyone who worked could attend in their lunch-time, he preached his last ever sermon, '*The Kingdom of heaven is at hand; repent ye, and believe the gospel*.' Under that ash tree, known today as the Wesley tree, '*the Word was with mighty power and the tears of the people flowed in torrents*'.

I love open-air work. There is nothing like going onto the streets and proclaiming the gospel. I have personally seen hundreds become Christians through open-air ministry. There are many other benefits as well:

- You will raise the profile of Jesus: '*But I, when I am lifted up from the earth, will draw all men to myself*' (John 12:32). The Greek verb *hupsoo* for 'lifted up' is used literally but also metaphorically, in the sense of exalting the name of Jesus. This is what we do when we lift his name up on the streets, and it has tremendous power.
- You are able to reach people who aren't Christians. If they don't come to us, then we should go to them. You can reach large numbers very effectively – it really is not unusual to reach several hundred during a two-hour open-air session.
- It will significantly raise the profile of your church. Your church should be part of your community, so let your community know about you. This is often much harder for some of the 'new' churches that don't have a permanent building or specific place of worship. Going onto the streets will let people know that you are there for them.
- You will smash misconceptions of Christians being boring and miserable, by demonstrating fun, friendship and life. That's why Jesus came, to give us life: '*I have come that they may have life, and have it to the full*' (John 10:10). Go and demonstrate the abundant life that you have received so others might find it so attractive that they'll want it too.
- Working on the streets will build faith in you and give you and your team the opportunity to pray for people, perform and preach – maybe for the first time.

I'm sure you can think of many other benefits of doing open-air work. There are many different types and ways of doing it. Once again, what follows isn't a comprehensive guide, but ideas and thoughts to whet your appetite. Here are some of the things I have been involved with over the years and I know work.

Detached

This is open-air evangelism without props. You simply find out where people are and go out in pairs and chat to them, building friendships and showing care and concern that will practically demonstrate the love of God. Five things to bear in mind when undertaking detached work:

- Research – before you and your partner go out for the first time, do a quick recce to see who is out and about, and more importantly where. Perhaps in the week, your local young people hang about outside the local chip shop. They're there every evening from around 7 p.m. until 10 p.m. – just imagine the kind of impact you could have on these young lives, meeting with them on a consistent basis. You could, after all, be the only example of a real Christian they'll ever meet.
- Friends first – relax and enjoy your times out on the streets. Of course it can be daunting going out for the first time and striking up a conversation with a complete stranger, but it is such an effective way of reaching people who wouldn't necessarily come to you. So relax. The PA system, sketch board and daft props are safe in the lock-up, so take it easy and have fun making new friends and sowing seeds. Believe that you'll see the fruit of all this sowing in time.
- Commitment – allow me to stress the point again – friendships take time, so when you have a particularly good contact, follow it up by agreeing to meet again. Successful detached work demands a regular commitment. Perhaps the young people you are working with are really into skating, for example. Now you might not have ever been on a skateboard or roller skates in your life, so don't feel that to reach this group you need to rush out and buy all the gear and equipment so you can be part of their gang too. You'll probably look very silly and could make more enemies than friends. But if that group always had hassle from local people who

objected to their skating around their streets, you'd be better seeing how you could help them really practically. Perhaps you could work with the council in trying to find them a place to skate, or getting some money together to build some ramps, or whatever. They'll soon start to ask why you're doing it. As my mate, Nick Mitchell, who works for Youth for Christ in London, says: '*Sometimes young people don't need another mate. They need someone to fight their corner.*'

- Be sensible – there is a great strength in going in pairs, and it makes approaching a large group a little easier. However, two people approaching a single person could appear threatening, so be flexible and sensitive on this one. For obvious reasons it's not ideal for a lad to chat to a girl one-on-one, or the other way around. Your intentions may be perfectly pure and godly, but the person you're talking to may not have quite the same intentions! It's not a good idea for a couple of girls to approach a large group of lads and vice versa, so I favour having a male and female in each team.

- Be open to God – approaching complete strangers and talking to them could be the ideal moment for you to use spiritual gifts. Ask God to reveal things about the people you're conversing with. That's what Jesus did in his encounter with the woman at the well (John 4) and it had a major effect.

Praise and worship

Praise and worship have always played a significant part in revivals through history, and throughout the Bible, praise and worship are linked in the context of warfare. We can read one such instance in the Old Testament when Judah was confronted by mortal enemies, Moab and Ammon. Jehoshaphat sent musicians out in front of his army and the result of the praise and worship was victory:

> After consulting the people, Jehoshaphat appointed men to sing to the LORD and to praise him for the splendour of his holiness as they went out at the head of the army, saying: 'Give thanks to the LORD, for his love endures for ever.' As

they began to sing and praise, the LORD set ambushes against the men of Ammon and Moab and Mount Seir who were invading Judah, and they were defeated. (2 Chronicles 20:21–2)

When you worship in your streets, precincts and parks you engage in spiritual warfare – and it's great! It will build faith in you and your team and we've seen already what happens when we lift Jesus up – John 12:32 – he'll draw all men, women, boys and girls to himself. It'll also give you an opportunity to hear from God, and something of his heart and compassion for the area you're in and the people there.

Surveys and questionnaires

The benefits of these have already been mentioned in the chapter on door-to-door work. I've also included a sample Community Survey and Beliefs Questionnaire as Appendixes 1 and 2 at the back of this book. Once again these are really tools to get you chatting to people, which could well steer you onto a conversation about Jesus.

In the past I've often used one question on a large board set up in the middle of a precinct. Something daft like: 'Do you believe in the Loch Ness Monster?' I've kept score of people's responses, and it's not unusual for passers-by to stop their shopping and come over to give their opinion. As I've just said, it's another tool to steer you onto asking about more important views, opinions and beliefs.

If you're using a survey or questionnaire, then have it properly printed and secure it onto a clipboard. Work in pairs and take it in turns to ask the questions. Have a small gift, maybe a good-quality, glossy Gospel – which of course has been pre-printed with your church's contact details – for everyone who takes the time and trouble to be surveyed.

Literature

This could be either invitational or an explanation of the gospel. The first would probably be an invitation to a special guest event at your church, or a brochure advertising your church. Don't forget the date, time of start *and* finish, location (with perhaps a map), price (if applicable), contact phone number and a brief description of the event/s.

The second form of literature would be an accessible explanation of the gospel. It could be a personal story tract – more about this later – or a simple, well-illustrated and well-produced gospel explanation.

Drama

Good drama is an excellent form of communication. It will appeal to all ages and backgrounds, and can draw and hold huge crowds. I certainly don't claim to be an expert on drama, but from experience I have learned a few things:

- Rehearse well – performances on the streets are a shop window of what church and Christianity is all about. So make your sketches good and polished.
- Smash misconceptions – demonstrate fun and life, and show what Christianity is really like, smashing loads of misconceptions in the process.
- Make one point – make your drama short, sweet and punchy, after all you're not putting in an Oscar-winning performance. Perhaps focus on the effects of sin, or Jesus. Don't make it an epic of *Ben Hur* proportions. Remember KISS – Keep It Short and Sweet.
- Keep dialogue to a minimum – if you don't have a PA system, which you probably won't on the majority of occasions, you don't want the crowd to miss your point because they can't hear the words. Keep the dialogue to an absolute minimum.
- Leave the crowd with an image that will stick in their mind – good drama, well done, will stick in people's minds. It's true

that a picture is worth a thousand words, so leave good, fun, positive pictures with your audience.

Preaching

When you preach in the open air, you only have a few minutes to share your message, so think clearly what you're going to say and what you're not going to say. Keep it simple and straightforward. We've looked already at effective ways of communicating the good news, so maybe use the God, Sin, Jesus, Faith framework.

Be as natural as you can be and build a rapport with your listeners; after all communication isn't just what you say, it's how you say it. Your appearance, attitude and demeanour speak volumes too. Expect to feel nervous but take encouragement in the following words from John Wesley: '*Give me 100 preachers who fear nothing but sin and desire nothing but God, and I care not a straw whether they be clergymen or laymen; they alone will shake the gates of hell and set up the kingdom of heaven on earth.*' You can have a huge impact.

Presentation

This is a mix of probably all of the above and is what I personally enjoy doing best, because it's so much fun and changes lives in the process. The programme will be short – fifteen to twenty minutes absolute maximum – and will be fast-moving, humorous, will grab attention and have the gospel message threaded throughout. Because the crowd will change, you should run the programme a few times, and use the time in between for conversations.

A good programme might run like this:

Praise and worship	5 minutes
Introduction	1 minute
Drama	3 minutes
Testimony	2 minutes
Drama	3 minutes
Preach	2 minutes

Don't forget

- The praise and worship at the beginning of the programme isn't there necessarily to draw a crowd, though invariably it will. Instead it is for the team to focus on God, and build faith.
- At the end of your worship, your team becomes rent-a-crowd and forms a nice, loose semicircle that looks in at your compère, who welcomes the crowd and looks after proceedings.
- Talk to people whenever you can – it's much better than just handing out leaflets.
- Take plenty of mints with you for those who may have enjoyed a curry or a loaf of garlic bread the night before!
- The drama needs to be good and well-rehearsed. Because of its appeal to all ages and backgrounds, creative performances can be powerful methods of communication, and will leave images that stick in the mind for a long time.
- Put one person in charge of all props, their delivery, return and safekeeping during your time on the streets. Similarly, have someone else in charge of all publicity materials, tracts, Gospels, questionnaires, clipboards, pens and anything else you might need.
- Don't give out literature or interrupt people while they're still watching the presentation.
- At the end of the preaching your team immediately gets into conversations with the audience and asks them what they thought of the presentation.
- Smile and enjoy it!
- Expect people to become Christians.

Some final thoughts

The law

It is our constitutional right, under English common law, to present the gospel on the streets. We are guaranteed freedom of speech and assembly in public places, which of course includes most streets, roads, pavements, parks and most shopping centres. I use the word 'most' because over the years, many local councils have passed bylaws to limit what happens on the streets. Also, some privately owned shopping centres will not allow you access.

The major problem I have encountered is that of obstruction, so the choice of your venue is an important factor. You might be moved on if you cause an obstruction. In practice, I have found that the police very rarely take any action unless the blockage you and your audience are causing is fairly major.

You will normally need permission to use a PA system, but even if this is granted you need to be sensitive that you are not 'disturbing the peace', otherwise once again you could be asked to stop. With training and practice you will be able to learn how to project your voice well without the help of PA. Indeed I was once moved on for disturbing the peace in Leicester Square in Central London, and that was without a microphone and amplifier! Finally on the subject of the law, if you have obtained written permission for your open-air event, then make sure you have it with you, just in case of any problems.

Hecklers

I'm always getting heckled and I have to admit, most of the time I really enjoy it! There was one time, however, at a large event at Plymouth University when it started to get on my nerves. For my full forty-five-minute performance one lad interrupted and heckled me continually. I carried on undaunted, using my best and most rehearsed ad libs (that's a contradiction if ever I heard one) and presented the gospel message to the best of my ability. I came off-stage to find this very same lad sat at my table, grinning from ear to ear, having bought me a pint of lager. 'You were great,' he said. 'I heckle everyone and you did a great job. It didn't faze you one bit, did it?' I took all this as a compliment, though for one fleeting moment I couldn't decide whether to drink the pint or tip it over his head – in love you understand!

I have found from experience that most hecklers fall into two categories: humorous or drunk. They are almost always good-natured though, and you can use their interaction to great effect. It's well worth practising, rehearsing and filing at the back of your mind a selection of nice, humorous retorts to hecklers. Of course you and I know that you've prepared them in advance, but your audience will think you're incredibly quick-witted and will listen to what else you have to say. A few of my favourite put-down lines would be along the following lines:

- He's a legend in his own lunch-time.
- Are you a figment of your own imagination?
- I heard a lot about you. Now I'd like to hear your side.
- Please save all the questions until I leave.
- I'll provide the dialogue.
- I don't bother you when you're working.
- Hey, you're the guy who heckled me ten years ago. I never forget a suit.
- I'm sorry, I couldn't hear you, I was talking.
- Did your brains come with instructions?
- Sir, you have a ready wit. Let me know when it's ready.

Well, I hope all of that helps. The streets and precincts of our nation contain fertile ground, so let's get out there and sow some seed, and believe God to do some serious reaping. Jesus always believed God for great things: '*Everything is possible for him who believes*' (Mark 9:23). The early Church was certainly up for it so let's go and make a difference in the open air.

Prayer

A tourist came too close to the edge of the Grand Canyon, lost his footing and plunged over the side, clawing and scratching to save himself. After he went out of sight and just before he fell into space, he saw a bush, which he desperately grabbed with both hands. Filled with terror, he called out toward heaven, 'Is there anyone up there?'

A calm, powerful voice came out of the sky, 'Yes, there is.'

The tourist pleaded, 'Can you help me? Can you help me?'

The calm voice replied, 'Yes, I probably can. What is your problem?'

'I fell over the cliff and am dangling in space holding to a bush that is about to break. Please help me.'

The voice from above said, 'I'll try. Do you believe?'

'Yes, yes, I believe.'

'Do you have faith?'

'Yes, yes. I have strong faith.'

The calm voice said, 'Well, in that case, simply let go of the bush and everything will turn out fine.'

There was a tense pause, then the tourist yelled, 'Is there anyone else up there?'

God loves to answer our prayers though it's not always in the way we expect. I do feel we sometimes need to remind ourselves that prayer isn't about twisting God's arm, hoping that he will give us what we want. The well-known evangelist Billy Graham admitted, '*The only time my prayers aren't answered are on the golf course!'* Prayer is about relationship-building and discovering God's agenda, not ours. The Bible says this:

> Ask and it will be given to you; seek and you will find; knock and the door will be opened to you. For everyone who asks receives; he who seeks finds; and to him who knocks, the door will be opened. (Matthew 7:7–8)

Uppermost on that agenda is God's relationship with people and it's in that context, particularly, that we're going to examine prayer in this chapter.

It is no accident that most of the great awakenings in history have begun in prayer. A prayer meeting under a haystack in a rainstorm in 1806 led to the first large-scale American missionary efforts. In 1830 some 30,000 people were converted in Rochester, New York, under the ministry of Charles Finney. Later Finney said the reason was the faithful praying of one man who never attended the meetings but gave himself to prayer. In 1872, the American evangelist Dwight L. Moody began a gospel campaign in London, which was used by God to touch countless lives. Later Moody discovered that a 'humble, bedridden girl' had been praying.

In May 1934 a North Carolina farmer lent a pasture to some thirty local businessmen who wanted to devote a day of prayer for the city of Charlotte because the Depression had spread spiritual apathy there. They had planned, despite the indifference of local ministers, to hold an evangelistic campaign later that year. During that day of prayer on the farmland their leader, Vernon Patterson, prayed that 'out of Charlotte the Lord would raise up someone to preach the gospel to the ends of the earth'. The businessmen next built in the city a large church of pine on a steel frame, where for eleven weeks from September 1934 a renowned, fiery Southern evangelist named Mordecai Fowler Ham and his song leader, Walter Ramsay, shattered the complacency of churchgoing Charlotte. Well, God did hear their prayer. The farmer who lent his pasture for the prayer meeting was Franklin Graham and his son Billy became a Christian during the meetings. The rest is history.

In 1993, Paul Ariga, a key church leader from Japan, visited Argentina and received a special anointing for intercessory prayer. Upon his return to Japan, he recruited 13,000 fellow intercessors who collectively prayed for 350,000 hours for the lost in Japan. As a result, 125,000 people heard the gospel and 22,000 became Christians.

During the Global March for Jesus in London, on 25 June 1994, some 75,000 people gathered in Hyde Park and took a few moments to pray for Bangladesh. They prayed for those in authority, the local and national government, for teachers, police and the military. In small groups, people prayed specifically for the salvation of the 116 million people of one of the world's poorest nations, and the spreading of the gospel. Together the 75,000 proclaimed: 'Lord, make your name great in Bangladesh. Let the people of Bangladesh be saved and come to a knowledge of the truth.' Some years later, missionaries in Bangladesh were asked if they'd noticed any changes in the country. They started to list a whole catalogue of incredible changes, and the date they could trace these changes back to was 25 June 1994.

We shouldn't really be surprised by these wonderful stories, because we know that God can change things through prayer. James, an early church leader, encourages us to keep praying and not give up with these words:

> The prayer of a righteous man is powerful and effective. Elijah was a man just like us. He prayed earnestly that it would not rain, and it did not rain on the land for three and a half years. Again he prayed, and the heavens gave rain, and the earth produced its crops. (James 5:16–18).

That's pretty powerful praying.

It stands to reason that if God can turn whole nations around, then he can most certainly do it with individuals, so it should be key in all our evangelistic endeavours. Eric Delve, who I consider to be one of the finest evangelists in Britain, said this:

> I think the most powerful thing we can do to draw people into our relationship with Jesus is to offer prayer at the

right moment. Frequently Christian people are asked to 'Say one for me will you?' and I have always at that moment said, 'Yes, of course,' grabbed them by the elbow (because we fend people off with our elbow, it is the least offensive thing to hold them by) and immediately pray for whatever need it is that they've told us about. By the time I have finished praying they have just worked out that is what I am doing, and since real prayer is a two-way thing, they've become aware not only that I was talking, but that some-body else was listening and responding. I know of no more effective method of witness than simply praying for somebody.

The prayer checklist that follows might just help to get you praying more effectively:

Be specific

John Wesley, the founder of the Methodist Church said: '*It seems God is limited by our prayer life – that he can do nothing for humanity unless someone asks him.*' If that's the case, let's ask him to intervene in situations, in very specific ways. Vague prayers get vague answers, so it follows that specific prayers get specific answers, so:

- Pray for individuals by name;
- Pray for their family;
- Ask God to bless their friendship with you;
- Pray that their opinion of Christianity might change positively;
- Pray for their needs; and
- Pray for opportunities to share more of the gospel with them.

Pray with others

It helps to keep the discipline going if you pray with others. You can also encourage each other as God answers your prayers. Billy Graham told in his autobiography, *Just As I Am*, of the prayer groups that specifically prayed for his visit to England in 1954.

I reported to the audience that prayer groups all over the world were focusing their attention on London for these meetings – including, we heard 35,000 groups in India. Now that was newsworthy! All our preparation, promotion, and programming, and even my preaching itself – necessary as those things were – were nothing compared with the prayer power around the world.

Pray for boldness

'*Now, Lord, consider their threats and enable your servants to speak your word with great boldness*' (Acts 4:29). This boldness or *parrhesia* is not a human quality but comes from God. God is the source of power, so ask him for more of it. Ask God for the boldness to see breakthroughs in your evangelism and believe for specific opportunities.

Pray for the workers

'*Brothers, pray for us*' (1 Thessalonians 5:25). The gospel first reached Europe around AD 49. These words asking for prayer came from Paul and his team of Silvanus and Timothy. These men were pioneers with the gospel but were still in desperate need of the prayers of their brothers and sisters in Christ. Your prayers could make all the difference for those out on the front line in evangelism today. While ministering in Mexico in 2000, my friend Anthony Delaney was leading a large prayer meeting in Canterbury Cathedral. At the close of the meeting the 1,200-strong congregation were asked to pray specifically for my ministry in Mexico that week. I tell you this, it made a huge difference to the impact we had in that country during our trip.

Pray for more workers

'*He told them, "The harvest is plentiful, but the workers are few. Ask the Lord of the harvest, therefore, to send out workers into his harvest field"* ' (Luke 10:2). We need to see more people doing evangelism if we are to reach our vast world of 6.12 billion people.

After years of faithful Christian service in South Africa, the famous missionary Robert Moffat returned to Scotland to recruit helpers. When he arrived at the church one cold wintry night, he was dismayed that only a small group had come out to hear him. What bothered him even more was that the only people in attendance were women. Although he was grateful for their interest, he had hoped particularly to challenge the men in the village. He was so discouraged that he almost failed to notice one small boy in the loft, who was pumping away at the bellows of the organ. Moffat felt frustrated as he gave his message, for he realised that very few women could be expected to undergo the particularly hard life in undeveloped jungles. But God works in mysterious ways.

Although no one volunteered that evening, the young lad assisting the organist was deeply moved by the challenge. As a result, he promised God he would follow in the footsteps of this pioneer missionary. And he remained true to his vow. When he grew up, he went and ministered to the unreached tribes of Africa. The young man's name was David Livingstone. Moffat never ceased to wonder that his appeal, which he had intended for men, had stirred a young boy, who eventually became a mighty man of God.

Pray without ceasing

The Bible exhorts and requests us to '*pray continually*' until we see breakthrough (1 Thessalonians 5:17). In the classic movie *The Sound of Music* the Mother Superior warbled to Julie Andrews' unsuccessful nun familiar yet poignant lyrics, '*Climb every mountain, ford every stream, follow every rainbow, 'til you find your dream.*' These are indeed wise words. Keep going with your praying whatever the circumstances and certainly don't just pray when you feel like it. Sir Winston Churchill was a stubborn and determined man; he declared: '*Never give in! Never give in! Never! Never! Never! Never! In anything great or small, large or petty – never give in except to convictions of honour and good sense.*' Keep going!

Pray with faith

Now to him who is able to do immeasurably more than all we ask or imagine, according to his power that is at work within us, to him be glory in the church and in Christ Jesus throughout all generations, for ever and ever! (Ephesians 3:20)

Believe for the impossible. God can do extraordinary things, over and above that which we can only dream of. Let's believe it. In the words of Oswald Chambers:

It is a great thing to be a believer, but easy to misunderstand what the New Testament means by it. It is not that we believe Jesus Christ can do things, or that we believe in a plan of salvation. It is that we believe him; whatever happens we will hang on to the fact that he is true.

Pray for compassion

Jesus was clearly set apart yet he never separated himself from human beings and their needs. Nor did he limit his concern to the spiritual part of people's personality. He had deep compassion for their welfare. Ask God to give you more compassion for the lost. Former American President, Woodrow Wilson, told this story. He said:

I was in a very common place, I was sitting in a barber chair, when I became aware that a personality had entered the room. A man had come quietly in upon the same errand as myself – to have his hair cut – and sat in the chair next to me. Every word the man uttered showed a personal interest in the man who was cutting his hair. And before I got through with what was being done for me, I was aware that I had attended an evangelistic service. Because Mr D. L. Moody was in that chair. I purposely lingered in the room after he had left and noted the singular effect that his visit had brought upon the barbershop. They didn't know his name but they knew that something had elevated their thoughts and I felt that I left that place as I should have left the place of worship. My admiration and esteem for Mr Moody became very deep indeed.

Pray for open doors

'*And pray for us, too, that God may open a door for our message, so that we may proclaim the mystery of Christ, for which I am in chains. Pray that I may proclaim it clearly, as I should*' (Colossians 4:3–4). I've mentioned throughout this book the principle of praying for 'divine appointments'. I guarantee that God will answer your prayers, and will arrange divine connections with individuals. Be 'on the ball' when it comes to recognising them!

Pray for revival

'*Sow for yourselves righteousness, reap the fruit of unfailing love, and break up your unploughed ground; for it is time to seek the LORD, until he comes and showers righteousness on you*' (Hosea 10:12). Don't just pray for nice meetings and handfuls of souls coming into the kingdom. Let's pray for revival – a sovereign move of God in our nation and throughout the world. Paul Yonggi Cho, in his book *Prayer, Key to Revival*, wrote: '*I am convinced that revival is possible anywhere people dedicate themselves to prayer . . . it has been historically true that prayer has been the key to every revival in the history of Christianity.*'

At the beginning of 2001, crowds of up to 6 million in Nigeria flocked to hear German evangelist Reinhard Bonnke. Organisers estimated that 1.6 million people poured into the crusade ground for the final meeting of the six-day Millennium Crusade, smashing all previous attendance records for Bonnke. Two thousand churches from scores of denominations joined forces to help stage the African event. They trained 200,000 counsellors and provided 25,000 ushers and security workers. Christ for all Nations (CfaN) shipped in thirty containers full of materials, including 6 million booklets for new converts. Reinhard Bonnke said that the success of the Lagos crusade was the fulfilment of a twenty-year-old prophecy: '*He said I would see more than 1 million souls saved in a single service – not just attendances, but salvations.*' Now that's what I call 'revival'.

I hope that list of suggestions will help you. Prayer is such a powerful thing and is such a key part of winning our friends, family and neighbours to Christ. The brilliant scientist Sir Isaac Newton once said that he could take his telescope and look millions and millions of miles into space. Then he added:

> But when I lay it aside, go into my room, shut the door, and get down on my knees in earnest prayer, I see more of heaven and feel closer to the Lord than if I was assisted by all the telescopes on earth.

Questions

Bob Marley used to wail that old familiar song, 'There are more questions than answers' and he makes a good point. One of the main reasons that I've found stops Christians sharing their faith is a fear of being asked a tough question about Christianity that they feel they won't be able to answer. They often feel their inability to provide a half-decent answer might in turn put the questioner off Christianity for ever. I have to admit we all feel that from time to time.

But I've got some good news and bad news for you. Let's get the bad news out of the way for starters by saying that unbelievers do have the rather irritating habit of asking us Christians pretty tough questions about our faith. Sometimes these questions are 'red herrings' to try to throw us off the real issues, while at other times the questions are very real and indeed are often asked from a genuine and searching heart. So, that's the bad news.

The good news is that most people tend to ask the same questions, so if we do some research and try to find some sort of answer to the most commonly asked questions then that will help us in our faith-sharing. We don't want to come across as some smart-Alec, know-it-all Christian, but as normal people who have thought out what we believe and why we believe in God. From my experience these are the most commonly asked questions.

- Who made God?
- How can you believe in something you can't see?

- Did Jesus really exist?
- How do you explain the resurrection?
- What about creation and evolution?
- Hasn't science disproved God?
- Isn't the Bible full of mistakes and contradictions?
- What about suffering?
- What about other religions?
- Isn't Christianity just a crutch?
- Won't a good life do?
- What about all the hypocrites in the Church?

Here follow some simple answers that are certainly not exhaustive. There are some great books available (some are mentioned in the Bibliography) that expand and improve on these outline answers. I do think simplicity and honesty are the best policy in our answers. Try to pack them with personal experience as no one can really argue with that, padded with Bible references and up-to-date illustrations that your questioner will understand and relate to. Finally, always try to turn the answer and refocus the conversation onto Jesus. Here we go . . .

Who made God?

When I was at school I always used to have an image of God as an old Father Christmas lookalike, with a bushy white beard, going thin on top and wearing a Marks and Spencer nightshirt. I don't know what images are conjured up in your mind. Maybe they're similar, maybe not. But if there is a God in heaven somewhere, how on earth did he get there? And for that matter, who made him?

The answer's short and sweet. No one! I believe God's always been there and always will be there. In the eighteenth century the philosopher Jean Jacques Rousseau attempted to describe it like this:

> I know nothing of his having created matter, bodies, spirits or the world. The idea of creation confounds me and surpasses my conception, though I believe as much of it as

I am able to conceive. But I know that God has formed the universe and all that exists, in the most consummate order. He is doubtless eternal, but I am incapacitated to conceive an idea of eternity. All that I can conceive is that he existed before all things, that he exists with them and will exist after them, if they should ever have an end.

Now the statement that God has always been there and will always be there might be a bit of a strange concept to get our tiny minds around. After all, everything needs to be created. Yes, that's certainly true for physical things like the chair I'm sitting on at this very minute, or the keyboard that I'm thumping away at to write this book. But the Bible says God is *spiritual*, not *physical*. '*He existed before everything else began, and he holds all creation together*' (Colossians 1:17, New Living Translation).

So, it's not outside the realms of possibility to suggest that spiritual beings don't have to obey physical laws, and in fact exist totally outside of these laws. Professor Sir Ghillean Prance, who was a Director of the Royal Botanical Gardens at Kew in London, said: '*Physical laws came into being because there is a Creator who made them.*'

I hope that this has given part of an answer to this tricky question. Let me leave the last word to Andre Gide, the French Nobel Prize-winning author, who said this: '*I cannot tell where God begins, still less where he ends. But my belief is better expressed if I say that there is no end to God's beginning.*'

How can you believe in something you can't see?

Eugene Crenan, one of the American astronauts who enjoyed the exciting experience of walking on the moon, said with wonder as he looked at our planet from space:

Our world appears big and beautiful, all blue and white! You can see from the Antarctic to the North Pole. The earth looks so perfect. There are no strings to hold it up; there is no fulcrum upon which it rests.

Contemplating the infinity of time and space, he said he felt as if he were seeing the earth from God's perspective.

As we've already said, of course you can't see God. Or for that matter, taste, touch or smell him. But so what? Sometimes you just have to believe in things that you can't see. There's electricity, for example. You can't see it, though you can see the effect of it, when you turn on a light switch. Then there are radio waves – you just know when you turn on your radio that sound is going to come out. What about microwaves? You can't see those either, but I know full well that when I put my half-eaten, cold, chicken vindaloo from the night before into the microwave to heat up, five minutes later it's piping hot and goes down a treat.

In the same way, although we can't physically see God, we can see the effects of God all around us, in the wonders of creation, for example. An article Jim Bishop wrote for the *Miami Herald*, and which follows here, says it much better than I could:

There is no God. All of the wonders around us are accidental. No almighty hand made a thousand stars. They made themselves. No power keeps them on their steady course. The earth spins itself to keep the oceans from falling off towards the sun. Infants teach themselves to cry when they are hungry or hurt. A small flower invented itself so that we could extract digitalis for sick hearts.

The earth gave itself day and night, and tilted itself so that we get seasons. Without the magnetic poles man would be unable to navigate the trackless oceans of water and air, but they grew there. How about the sugar thermostat in the pancreas? It maintains a level of sugar in the blood sufficient for energy. Without it, all of us would fall into a coma and die.

Why does snow sit on mountain-tops waiting for the warm spring sun to melt it at just the right time for the young crops in farms below to drink? A very lovely accident.

The human heart will beat for seventy to eighty years or more without faltering. How does it get sufficient rest between beats? A kidney will filter poison from the blood, and leave good things alone. How does it know one from the other?

Who gave the human tongue flexibility to form words, and a brain to understand them, but denied it to animals? Who showed a womb how to take the love of two people and keep splitting a tiny ovum until, in time, a baby would have the proper number of fingers, eyes and ears and hair in the right places, and come into the world when it is strong enough to sustain life?

There is no God?

Enough said.

Did Jesus really exist?

Barry Norman, the British film critic, made a profound statement when he was reviewing a movie about the life of Jesus.

> Very few people could have as magnetic a personality as Christ, and no actor has that. You will always know you are looking at an actor pretending to be someone infinitely greater than he is . . . The whole point about Christ, if you believe in Christ, is that Christ is divine, not that he was a jolly good chap.

We know that Jesus lived. He was a man in history, as well as a man for today. Tacitus, perhaps the greatest Roman historian, born in the first century, speaks of Jesus. Josephus, a Jewish historian, tells of the crucifixion of Jesus. A contemporary Bible scholar said that 'the latest edition of the *Encyclopaedia Britannica* uses 20,000 words in describing this person, Jesus. His description took more space than was given to Aristotle, Cicero, Alexander, Julius Caesar, Buddha, Confucius, Mohammed or Napoleon Bonaparte.'

Jesus was certainly something special. Let's look at just some of the evidence for his existence from three very different sources.

Jewish historians

The most famous of these is Josephus who was born around AD 37 in Jerusalem. He devoted a large part of his life to writing numerous books on the history of the Jews. One of these said this:

> Now there was about this time Jesus a wise man, if it be lawful to call him a man; for he was a doer of wonderful works, a teacher of such men as received the truth with pleasure. He drew over to him many Jews, and also many of the Gentiles. This man was the Christ. And when Pilate had condemned him to the cross, those who had loved him from the first did not forsake him for he appeared to them alive on the third day, the divine prophets having spoken these and thousands of other wonderful things about him. And even now, the race of Christians, so named from him, has not died out. (*Antiquities of the Jews*, XVIII, III)

Pagan writers

These unbelieving authors write about Jesus too. Tacitus, a Roman historian, for example, in AD 112 writes about the reign of the Emperor Nero and refers to Jesus and the Christians in Rome (*Annals*, XV, 44). Soon after this Pliny the Younger, once described as one of the world's great letter-writers, penned an interesting letter about Christianity to the Emperor Trajan. In it he mentions the early Christians singing hymns, worshipping Jesus as God, and pledging themselves not to do wicked things but instead to live moral lives. This is what he said:

> They were in the habit of meeting on a certain fixed day before it was light, when they sang in alternate verses a hymn to Christ, as to a god, and bound themselves by a solemn oath, not to do any wicked deeds, never to commit any fraud, theft or adultery, never to falsify their word, nor deny a trust when they should be called upon to deliver it up.

The Bible

Many would automatically discount the Bible as a form of reliable evidence because of its bias towards the Christian faith, or because it maybe has been added to, or exaggerated over the years – almost like a version of 'Chinese whispers'. But that's not so. Researchers in Israel, after subjecting the first five books of the Bible to exhaustive computer analysis, came to a different conclusion than even they had initially expected. Sceptics had long assumed the Torah (the first five books of the Bible) to have been the work of multiple authors, and not as Christians had always believed the work of one man, Moses.

But Scripture scholar Moshe Katz and computer expert Menachem Wiener of the Israel Institute of Technology discovered an intricate pattern of significant words in the books, spelled by letters separated at fixed intervals. The statistical possibilities of such patterns happening by chance would be one in three million. The material suggests a single, inspired author – in fact it could not have been put together by human capabilities at all. Adds Mr Wiener, 'So we need a non-rational explanation. And ours is that the Torah was written by God through the hand of Moses.'

How do you explain the resurrection?

Some years ago, Frank Morison, an American journalist, started to write a book to show that the resurrection never happened. After considerable research he realised that the resurrection really did happen, and he became a Christian. This is what Morison said in the introduction to his book, *Who Moved the Stone?*:

> This study is in some ways so unusual and provocative that the writer thinks it desirable to state here very briefly how the book came to take its present form. In one sense it could have taken no other, for it is essentially a confession, the inner story of a man who originally set out to write one kind of book and found himself compelled by the sheer force of circumstances to write another.

When we sit back and think about it logically I've got to admit that the resurrection just seems too impossible for words. But once again, our belief isn't merely based upon a vague religious feeling, but upon solid evidence to support it. The resurrection wasn't a first-century legend; it really did happen. Let's take a look at some arguments and suggestions as we try to unravel the five possible explanations for what might have happened over that first Easter weekend:

It was just a hallucination
Without getting too technical, a hallucination is the experience of seeing an object or event that is not actually present to the human senses. In other words, seeing something that isn't really there. I'm sure some people might hallucinate from time to time, but not hundreds in one go. Remember, after the resurrection, Jesus appeared to around 550 people, once to 500 in one go, but hallucinations only ever occur to certain individuals at a time.

I'm sure you can think of the major flaw in this supposed theory anyway. What happened to the body of Jesus? It was most definitely gone, no one ever disputed that. The resurrection was no hallucination.

The body was stolen
Some sceptics have suggested that someone stole his body – but who would do such a thing? Certainly not the Jews or the Romans. Within a matter of just weeks, all of Jerusalem was awash with rumours that Jesus had come back to life. Revolution was in the air on the basis of Jesus being alive. If the authorities had the body then why didn't they produce it to put an end to the rumours once and for all?

It is nigh on impossible to believe the disciples had taken it. They were terrified and were hiding out of the city. And anyway, how on earth did they get past well-trained and disciplined Roman guards? The guards would have faced the death penalty for losing a living prisoner, let alone a dead one! Why would they lie? What was the point? Remember most of the disciples went on to die for their belief that Jesus had come back to life – why die for a lie?

Maybe he never died

Others believe that Jesus fainted on the cross, miraculously revived in the tomb and simply passed himself off as having come back from the dead. Don't forget crucifixion was a common punishment, it was a slow and terrible form of death. History books tell us that in one day alone 6,000 men were crucified, so it was something the Romans were very good at. They certainly wouldn't have been sloppy enough to have let Jesus survive, especially as their governor Pontius Pilate had personally ordered his death. Jesus was dead, there was no doubt about it.

Anyway, think about it for a moment. Jesus had been brutally beaten, then endured a Roman scourging. He had been pinned upon a cross for six hours with nails in his hands and feet. A spear was rammed into his side piercing his heart. His dead body was then taken down and wrapped in yards of cloth soaked with spices and fragrances that would have hardened to around 34 kilograms. Then three days later, he woke up and managed to move a 1.5 to 2 tonne stone in front of an airtight tomb, fight his way past the Roman guard, and then walk miles to appear to his disciples as the conqueror of death. Need I say any more?

It was just a legend

This was no fairy story, we've already looked in detail at the evidence for this event from Jewish writers, Roman historians and the Bible itself. There's also overwhelming supporting evidence. Just one example to consider is the Garden Tomb that was discovered in 1885. General Gordon and his team were convinced that this was the place where the body of Jesus had lain. There is a traditional tomb inside the wall of the modern Jerusalem, but no certainty attaches to the site. This Garden Tomb, hidden for centuries, was covered with rubbish twenty feet high. When they first cleared the spot, with great caution they gathered all the dust and debris within the tomb and carefully shipped it to the Scientific Association of Great Britain. Every part of it was analysed, but there was no trace of human remains. If this was the real tomb of Jesus, then Jesus was the first to be laid there and he was also the last.

It was a miracle

The final option we have when we try to make sense of the resurrection is that it really did happen. John Singleton Copley, one of the great minds in British legal history and three times High Chancellor of England, wrote, '*I know pretty well what evidence is, and I tell you, such evidence as that for the resurrection has never broken down yet.*'

In the early part of the twentieth century, a group of lawyers met in England to discuss the biblical accounts of Jesus' resurrection. They wanted to see if sufficient information was available to make a case that would hold up in an English court of law. When their study was completed, they published the results of their investigations. They concluded that Jesus' resurrection was one of the most well-established facts of history.

Of course we can never prove scientifically that the resurrection happened, but we can most definitely prove the facts of history. When you logically think through the possible alternatives that have been offered, you can see major flaws in all their arguments. There's only one real alternative left, and that is that it actually happened as the Bible suggested. It was a miracle, because if God is God then why shouldn't he be able to do it? And the reason he did it was so that we could know him.

What about creation and evolution?

American author Charles Swindoll explained in his book, *Growing Deep in the Christian Life,* how we got cars:

Many centuries ago, all this iron, glass, rubber, fabric, leather and wires came up out of the ground. Furthermore, each substance fashioned itself into various shapes and sizes. Holes evolved in just the right places, and the upholstery began to weave itself together. After a while threads appeared on bolts and nuts, and amazing as it might sound, each bolt found nuts with matching threads. And gradually, everything sort of screwed up tightly in place. A little later, correctly shaped glass glued itself in the right places. And you see those tyres? They became round over the years.

And they found themselves the right sized metal wheels. And they sort of popped on. They also filled themselves with air somehow. And the thing began to roll down the street.

And one day, many, many years ago – centuries, really – some people were walking along and they found this vehicle sitting under a tree. And one of them looked at it and thought, 'How amazing! I think we should call it "automobile".' But there's more! These little automobiles have an amazing way of multiplying themselves year after year, even changing ever so slightly to meet the demands of the public.

We often seem to forget that the 'theory of evolution' is just that – a theory. Indeed, it is less of a scientific theory and more a philosophy about the origins of life and the meaning of humankind. But let me start off by making a distinction between *micro*- and *macro*- evolution. To me, micro-evolution makes sense, and basically means a variation and development within a species. For example, fish that live at the bottom of dirty lakes all their lives may lose the use of their sight completely over a period of millions of years. Macro-evolution, however, is completely different, and it means evolution from one species to another – the most famous example being orang-utans becoming human beings like you and me. To me that seems bananas! Something I'm sure the said orang-utans would appreciate! As such, macro-evolution is clearly contradictory to the Bible's account of creation.

The opening few verses of the Bible describe it like this:

In the beginning God created the heavens and the earth. Now the earth was formless and empty, darkness was over the surface of the deep, and the Spirit of God was hovering over the waters. And God said, 'Let there be light,' and there was light. (Genesis 1:1–3)

Christians as well as Jews and Muslims believe that God created the universe out of nothing, which seems very much at odds with the theory of evolution. But this theory isn't just at odds with the Bible, it also contradicts some very basic laws of science.

Scientists tell us about the second law of thermodynamics, a law of physics, which simply says that left to itself, everything tends to become less ordered, not more ordered or 'complex'. It's a pretty obvious law really, even to a non-scientist like myself: things grow old, run down, decay and eventually die. Batteries run out, your clothes get worn and faded, your trainers fall to bits, gadgets break – ultimately, everything falls apart – things do not get more complex or advanced, as the theory of evolution would suggest.

Always remember, evolution is not a fact. We are often under the impression that Christians are the only ones who don't believe in evolution. I can tell you that dozens of reputable secular scientists don't believe in evolution either. Professor Wickramasinghe the astronomer said this:

> The idea that life was put together by random shuffling of constituent molecules can be shown to be as ridiculous and improbable as the proposition that a tornado blowing through a junk yard may assemble a Boeing 747. The aircraft had a creator and so might life.

The atheist professor Richard Dawkins prefers to call living things 'designoid' to avoid the word 'designed'. But scientists are discovering that the vast universe is so complex that it is even more logical to believe in a Designer. The great Albert Einstein actually said this: 'Everyone who is seriously involved in the pursuit of science becomes convinced that a Spirit is manifested in the laws of the universe, a Spirit vastly superior to that of a man.' Years before that, Sir James Hopwood Jeans, the English physicist and mathematician stated, 'The universe seems to have been designed by a pure mathematician.'

The point is this: if God is God, than he would have no problem at all in creating the world exactly as is written in the Bible (Genesis 1–3). Many years ago, the famous scientist Sir Isaac Newton had an exact replica of the solar system made in miniature. At its centre was a large golden ball representing the sun, and revolving around it were small spheres attached at the ends by rods of varying lengths. They represented Mercury, Venus, Earth, Mars and all the other planets. These were all geared together by cogs and belts to make them move around the sun in perfect harmony.

One day as Newton was studying the model, a friend who did not believe in the biblical account of creation stopped by for a visit. Marvelling at the device and watching as the scientist made the heavenly bodies move on their own orbits, the man exclaimed, 'My, Newton, what an exquisite thing! Who made it for you?'

Without even looking up, Sir Isaac replied, 'Nobody.'

'Nobody?' replied his friend, puzzled.

'That's right! I said nobody! All of these balls, cogs, belts and gears just happened to come together, and wonder of wonders, by chance they began revolving in their set orbits with perfect timing.'

His friends soon got the message. It was plain stupid to suppose that the model just happened. But I think it is even more stupid to accept that the earth and the vast universe came into being by just chance. Isn't it more sensible and logical to accept what the Bible says, *'In the beginning, God created the heavens and the earth'* (Genesis 1:1)?

Hasn't science disproved God?

It is scientifically impossible to prove the existence of God, though I might add, it is scientifically impossible to *disprove* it too. You can't just put God in a test tube and analyse him in a laboratory. So sorry, I'm afraid there isn't any concrete proof that God lives.

Having said that, the Bible tells us that God exists. Christians believe that the Bible is much more than just a book; they believe that it is the actual *word of God*. Christians also believe that God exists because of Jesus, who was God in human form. The Bible says, *'The Word [Jesus] became human and lived here on earth among us'* (John 1:14, New Living Translation). The author goes on to tell us that *'he [Jesus] has told us about him [God]'* (John 1:18, New Living Translation).

We can look at our world, and human beings, animals, trees and the weather. Surely it couldn't have all happened by accident? Our world bears all the hallmarks of a creator. The human body, for instance, is a masterpiece of incredible design. Beautifully engineered, it is governed by several hundred systems of control – each interacting with and affecting the other. The brain has 10 billion nerve cells to record what a person sees and hears. The skin has more than 2 million tiny sweat glands – about 3,000 per square inch, all part of the intricate system that keeps the body at an even temperature. A 'pump' in the chest makes the blood travel 168 million miles a day – that's the equivalent of 6,720 times around the world! The lining of the stomach contains 35 million glands secreting juices that aid the process of digestion. And these are just a handful of the incredibly involved processes and chemical wonders that operate just to sustain life.

Science and Scripture do not automatically cancel each other out. They simply look at the world from different perspectives, which doesn't mean they necessarily contradict each other. Professor Albert Einstein said this: '*A legitimate conflict between science and religion cannot exist. Science without religion is lame, religion without science is blind.*'

Science can never prove that God is irrelevant to the universe. If God created it and set it up, as millions of Christians believe, then he is certainly *most* relevant! Science has never stopped belief in God, and many great scientists including Einstein, Edison, Newton, Boyle, Faraday, Pasteur, Kepler and Copernicus believed in God. Eighty years ago a survey of scientists revealed that 40 per cent believed in God. You might think that, with all the scientific breakthroughs and discoveries since that time, this figure might have changed quite drastically. But an identically worded survey recently published by the journal *Nature* arrived at an almost identical result – four out of ten scientists still believe in God.

An article in the journal *Science* in 1997 declared, '*Recent signs point towards a thaw in the ice between science and faith*', and in the summer of the following year the respected magazine *Newsweek* in its cover story proclaimed, '*Science Finds God.*' Back in the

UK, one modern British organisation, Christians in Science, has members and contacts numbering some 1,500 scientists, including university staff, scientists in industry and science teachers.

Remember, science asks *how* questions, Christianity asks *why*. The crux of the matter is this: the Bible isn't intended to be a science book, instead it's a book about a loving God who created people to be his friends. Adam and Eve mucked it up in Genesis, so God sent Jesus to make things right, so that we could know him again . . . if we want to.

Isn't the Bible full of mistakes and contradictions?

I often get asked this question when I'm working in schools. My immediate answer to the questioner is 'Which errors do you have in mind?' I can honestly say, with my hand on my heart, 99 times out of 100, the person can't think of any. They've heard someone else say that the Bible is full of mistakes, and they've swallowed the misconception hook, line and sinker!

Having said that, I have to admit that sometimes the Bible does *appear* to contradict itself, though time and time again, apparent contradictions have been explained by archaeological discoveries. Dr Nelson Glueck, an outstanding Jewish archaeologist, while writing his book, *Rivers in the Desert*, made this remarkable statement: '*No archaeological discovery has ever controverted a biblical reference.*' Bear in mind that this incredible statement came from one of the world's leading archaeologists.

Before we take a look at one supposed contradiction, let's look at an actual definition of the word 'contradiction'. It means 'a statement of the opposite'. For example, if the Bible says (which it doesn't) that Jesus died by strangulation, and that elsewhere Jesus instead died by being crucified, then that would be a contradiction.

Anyway, onto a supposed contradiction. It concerns the angels who were at the tomb of the crucified Jesus. The four Gospel writers seem to report differing accounts. Matthew and Mark relate that one angel spoke to the women, while Luke and John state that two angels were at the tomb. At first sight this would appear to be contradictory. However, Matthew and Mark didn't say there was only one angel at the tomb, but instead that one angel *spoke* to the women. You see the difference?

It's a little like the other week when I popped down to the Rustington Sports and Social Club with my mates Carl, Scott and Bruno. We had a couple of pints and had a chat with my other friends Arthur, Chris and Andrew. Someone mentioned to my wife that they'd seen me and Scott going into the club, then someone else mentioned that they'd seen me having an in-depth conversation over a pint and a bag of pork scratchings with Arthur. Now of course both of these witnesses were telling the truth, but these two accounts of my Sunday night out look completely different. They just came from different witnesses from different perspectives. Both statements, however, are completely true.

Anyway, back to the Bible. Although some of the details are different, which you would expect from different eye-witnesses, they agree on the important key points that Jesus was dead, buried and rose again. Wilbur Smith, a respected scholar, had this to say about the differences in the resurrection accounts:

> In these fundamental truths, there are absolutely no contradictions. The so-called variations in the narratives are only the details which were most vividly impressed on one mind or another of the witnesses of our Lord's resurrection, or on the mind of the writers of these four respective Gospels. The closest, most critical, examination of these narratives throughout the ages never has destroyed and can never destroy their powerful testimony to the truth that Christ did rise from the dead on the third day, and was seen of many.

What about suffering?

What a tough question! This is one we have to be so careful about answering, so try to delve a little deeper to ask why this question is being asked before you trot off some 'glib', clever answer. A friend of mine lost his baby son through a tragic cot

death a few years ago. He telephoned me in tears, asking 'Why?'
I couldn't give an answer, all I could do was pray and be a friend.
There seemed to be nothing to say.

Surely if God is as great, loving and caring as Christians make
out, why did their baby boy die, and why do so many innocent
people suffer? The whole suffering question is so hard to answer,
and sometimes even impossible. But let me try to give a few of
my perspectives on this subject.

First, I'd say if we're really honest, we have to take the blame
ourselves for most of the suffering in our world. Whenever a
child is abused, a senior citizen mugged, a person murdered you
have to point the finger at a human culprit, not God. The scientist
Albert Einstein blamed humankind for the evil in the world:
*'Evil is a problem in the hearts and minds of men. It is not a problem
of physics but of ethics. It is easier to denature [change the properties of]
plutonium than to denature the evil spirit of man.'*

Even natural disasters seem to be on the increase, as the world
seems quite literally to be falling apart. Yet God planned it to be
so different. In the beginning he wanted mankind to live in
friendship with him. Hardship, disease and suffering were not
on his agenda. I remember vividly in my teens watching the
BBC report from the famine in Ethiopia in 1985, and Bob
Geldof's comments as he stood and witnessed for himself the
devastation and said, *'Don't blame God, blame man.'* For only 200
miles away, in the capital Addis Ababa, vast amounts of money
were being spent on renovating homes for senior government
officials. More recently when Hurricane Mitch devastated
Nicaragua and Honduras, those unfortunate countries received
around US$5,000 a day from the West for hurricane relief, yet
had to pay back that very same figure, almost to the cent, in debt
repayments. The suffering adults and children were no better
off.

On a daily basis it seems, we turn on our televisions and see
people killed in earthquakes and tornadoes and other horrendous
natural disasters. In 1999 an earthquake that lasted just forty-five
seconds hit Turkey, killing 45,000 men, women, boys and girls.
The survivors didn't blame God; they blamed the Turkish
Government and they in turn blamed dishonest developers who

flaunted building regulations, cut corners and turned buildings into death-traps.

Ted Piedenbrock, an earthquake expert and structural engineer, sifted through the rubble in Turkey to find concrete that had been made with too much water, and also mixed with sea shells – a deadly short cut made to increase the profits of cowboy builders that even the Turkish authorities labelled as 'murderers'. Piedenbrock told the BBC, '*It is not very difficult or expensive to design structures that withstand virtually any size of earthquake with the minimisation of loss of life. The problem is allowing "cowboy" contractors to continue building.*' This so-called *natural* disaster was instead a *man-made* disaster.

But what of natural disasters that seem to occur so regularly and bring such pain and hardship? We can read in the book of Genesis how God gave people free will to love him, yet they chose to go their own way, and do their own thing. The world seemed to go wrong from that moment on. Christians call it the 'fall', scientists call it 'entropy' (from the second law of thermodynamics, which I mentioned earlier). Put simply, the world is in a state of decay and that's why earthquakes, typhoons, cyclones, whirlwinds, erupting volcanoes and the like cause so much damage today.

I have to say though that God is not detached from suffering, or indifferent to it. God tried to rectify the 'fall' by sending his one and only Son, Jesus, into the world to try to turn things around. An anonymous piece called 'The Long Silence' explains it like this:

Billions of people were scattered on a great plain before God's throne. Some of the groups near the front talked heatedly – not with cringing shame, but with belligerence. 'How can God judge us?' said one. 'What does he know about suffering?' snapped a young brunette. She jerked back a sleeve to reveal a tattooed number from a Nazi concentration camp. 'We endured terror, beatings, torture and death.'

In another group, a black man lowered his collar. 'What about this?' he demanded, showing an ugly rope burn.

'Lynched for no crime but being black! We have suffocated in slave ships, been wrenched from loved ones, toiled till death gave release.'

Far out across the plain were hundreds of such groups. Each had a complaint against God for the evil and suffering he permitted in his world. How lucky God was to live in heaven where there was no weeping, no fear, no hunger, no hatred.

Indeed, what did God know about what man had been forced to endure in this world? 'After all, God leads a pretty sheltered life,' they said. So each group sent out a leader, chosen because he had suffered the most. There was a Jew, a black person, an untouchable from India, an illegitimate person, a victim of Hiroshima and one from a Siberian slave camp.

In the centre of the plain, they consulted with each other. At last they were ready to present their case. It was rather simple: before God would be qualified to be their judge, he first must endure what they had endured. Their decision was that God should be sentenced to live on earth – as a man. But because he was God, they set certain safeguards to be sure he could not use any of his divine powers to help himself.

Let him be born a Jew. Let the legitimacy of his birth be doubted, so that none would know who his father was. Let him champion a cause so just, but so radical, that it brings down upon him the hate, condemnation and efforts of every major traditional and established religious authority to eliminate him.

Let him try to describe what no other man has ever seen, tasted, heard or smelled – let him try to communicate God to men. Let him be betrayed by his closest friends. Let him be indicted on false charges, tried before a prejudiced jury and convicted by a cowardly judge.

Let him see what it is to be terribly alone and completely abandoned by every living thing. Let him be tortured and let him die. Let him die the most humiliating death – with common thieves.

As each leader announced his portion of the sentence, loud murmurs of approval went up among the throngs of people. But when the last had finished pronouncing sentence, there was a long silence. No one uttered a word. No one moved. For suddenly all knew: God had already served his sentence.

That really is quite something. God has experienced suffering himself, and I believe can help us through life's problems and difficulties.

One night a man had a dream. He dreamed he was walking along the beach with God and across the sky flashed scenes from his life. For each scene, he noticed two sets of footprints in the sand; one belonging to him and the other to God.

When the last scene of his life flashed before him, he looked back at the footprints in the sand. He noticed that many times along the path of his life there was only one set of footprints. He also noticed that it happened at the very lowest and saddest times in his life.

This really bothered him and he questioned God about it. 'Lord, you said that once I decided to follow you, you'd walk with me all the way. But I have noticed that during the most troublesome times in my life, there is only one set of footprints. I don't understand why when I needed you most, you would leave me?'

God replied: 'My precious, precious child, I love you and would never leave you. During those times of trial and suffering, when you see only one set of footprints, it was then that I carried you.'

That story, written by an unknown author but called 'Footprints', is a wonderful encouragement. God is there for us in the good times and the bad times, because he loves and wants the best for us. He wants that wrong relationship at the 'fall' put right, which is possible because of what Jesus achieved through his death and resurrection.

What about other religions?

Don't all roads lead to God? I've heard that said hundreds of times. It's a bit like saying all roads lead to Rustington! Utter rubbish!! The assumption is that people from different religions are experiencing the same God, yet expressing it in different ways.

I really believe that can't be true. They're all so different. Let me give you one example, of Jesus' words on the subject of forgiveness. '*And when you stand praying, if you hold anything against anyone, forgive him, so that your Father in heaven may forgive you your sins*' (Mark 11:25).

Powerful and forgiving words from the founder of Christianity. Now compare that quotation with the words of Muslim leader Ayatollah Khomeini on the same subject of forgiveness, when he was talking about the author Salman Rushdie on the publication of his controversial book, *The Satanic Verses*. '*Even if Salman Rushdie repents and becomes the most pious man of all time, it is still incumbent on every Moslem to employ everything he's got to send him to hell.*' Do you notice the subtle difference?!

I do have to say though that most religions, including Islam, have elements of truth and some excellent moral teaching. But we need to look at the words of Jesus again. '*I am the way and the truth and the life. No-one comes to the Father except through me*' (John 14:6). You can't really argue with that. Christianity isn't about going to church twenty-five times on a Sunday, or watching *Songs of Praise*! Christianity is all about a personal relationship with God that is available only through his Son, Jesus. Christianity is unique because its founder is still alive. No other religion claims that. You can visit the graves of the founders of the others. Jesus is the only one who's still alive.

Isn't Christianity just a crutch?

Many people think Christianity is just a psychological crutch to get sad and weak people through the humdrum of life. So, is it a crutch? Well, the answer has to be 'yes' and 'no'.

Yes, because knowing Jesus helps us through our lives. We all endure hardships and elements of suffering – Jesus is there for us, and I believe can help us through the good times and the bad times. He's there for us. '*God has said, "Never will I leave you; never will I forsake you"* ' (Hebrews 13:5).

Then no, it's not a crutch, because as we've seen from the previous answers, Christianity isn't just a nice story like 'Postman Pat' or 'Snow White and the Seven Dwarfs' that cheers us up a bit when we're depressed. It's not like drugs or alcohol to perk us up temporarily when we're feeling down. Christianity is true! Jesus lived and was very real. An anonymous author made this striking comparison when comparing Jesus with others:

> His unique contribution to the race of men is salvation of the soul. Philosophy could not accomplish that. Nor art. Nor literature. Nor music. Only Jesus Christ can break the enslaving chains of sin and Satan. He alone can speak peace to the human heart, strengthen the weak, and give life to those who are spiritually dead.

So the answer to the original question is, I guess, 'Yes and no'. But either way, the Christian lifestyle isn't an easy option, but I've discovered that it is the best way to live your life.

Won't a good life do?

Unfortunately, the Bible doesn't allow anyone to earn their way into heaven. Of course it's great to do good, support charity, be nice to people and generally be kind and considerate. But the Bible makes it clear: whether we like it or not, our good works and deeds, while being very admirable, don't actually bring us into a relationship with God. '*He saved us, not because of righteous things we had done, but because of his mercy. He saved us through the washing of rebirth and renewal by the Holy Spirit*' (Titus 3:5).

Let me explain why just being good isn't enough. I guess it's all got to do with definitions. God's standard of '*good*' is perfection, and none of us can reach that. Even if we've never murdered anyone, or stolen goods from the supermarket, however good we think we might be, we don't come up to God's standards of perfection. Paul, when writing to the Christians in Rome, made it crystal clear: *'All have sinned; all fall short of God's glorious standard'* (Romans 3:23, New Living Translation).

Now that's pretty depressing really. There's nothing any of us can do to get good enough to get to God. Before you stick your head in the oven and turn the gas on, let me give you the good news. Paul carried on his letter: *'Yet now God in his gracious kindness declares us not guilty. He has done this through Christ Jesus, who has freed us by taking away our sins'* (Romans 3:24, New Living Translation).

The television presenter Anne Diamond was speaking on television about 'belief', and this is one of the comments she made: *'It doesn't matter what you believe, as long as you are sincere.'* I've got to say, and apologies to you Anne if you're reading this book, but that comment is utter hogwash! Sincerity has nothing to do with it at all. People can be sincerely wrong about things; does that make things right? I'm sure Adolf Hitler, in his own deranged mind, was sincere about wishing to create a master race, and annihilating 6 million Jewish men, women and children in the process. Those devastating results proved that he was most definitely sincerely wrong.

Sincerity and doing good simply aren't enough. That means good and bad people both need Jesus the same – whoever they are, whatever they've done, Jesus is the only way.

What about all the hypocrites in the Church?

The infamous outlaw Jesse James killed a man in a bank robbery and shortly afterwards was baptised in the Kearney Baptist Church in the USA. Then he killed another man, a bank cashier, and joined the church choir. Apparently Jesse loved Sundays, but didn't always have the time to attend church, as Sunday was the day he robbed trains. What a hypocrite!

Another reason many reject Christianity is because of hypocrisy in the Church. Once again, I have to admit that there are some hypocrites in the Church, as there are in all walks of life. Basically a hypocrite is a person who says one thing but does another.

As well as personal hypocrisy, there is also the more complicated form of hypocrisy of evil done throughout history in the name of Christianity; for example, the crusades, the inquisition and the terrible troubles in Northern Ireland. I have to admit that Christian history does have a dark side, but we do not have to admit that those who performed these evil actions were real Christians. To put it bluntly, their actions represent the very antithesis of what Jesus was all about.

Jesus hated all forms of hypocrisy. This is what he said, or should I say shouted, at a bunch of religious hypocrites one day:

> Woe to you, teachers of the law and Pharisees, you hypocrites! You clean the outside of the cup and dish, but inside they are full of greed and self-indulgence. Blind Pharisee! First clean the inside of the cup and dish, and then the outside also will be clean. (Matthew 23:25–6)

Jesus certainly got very angry about hypocrisy.

As I've said, unfortunately the church does have its fair share of hypocrites and has done throughout history. But that never invalidates the fact that the Christian message is true. Let me give you a personal example of what I mean by that.

I am a big fan of Indian food, and whenever I travel I always make the effort to sample local cuisine, and on an annual basis, make an award for my personal 'Indian Restaurant of the Year'. I was delighted to give the 1999 trophy to my local curry house, Tandoori Nights, in Rustington, and was pleased to feature in newspaper and local radio interviews about the award. I would tell all my friends about the quality of the food, the size of the portions and the friendly service. But could you imagine what would happen if I always ate my Indian food at other restaurants? You might say, 'What a hypocrite.' If I believed all that I'd said about Tandoori Nights, then I'd always eat my Indian cuisine there and nowhere else. Well, that's probably true (and in fact is, in this case!). Yet my being a hypocrite would not invalidate my claim that Tandoori Nights is the best. Do you see what I mean?

There are hypocrites everywhere in life and the Church is no exception. But we shouldn't write them all off. Just because there are a few football hooligans who seem hell-bent on violence and destruction it doesn't mean that every football supporter in the world is out for trouble. No Christians are perfect; we're all imperfect individuals at the end of the day. But that doesn't make us all hypocrites or frauds; it just makes us fallible people who need the help and forgiveness that Jesus offers. After all, if the great inventor Alexander Graham Bell had been arrested for shop-lifting, would that make using the telephone wrong? Of course not! I'm pleased to say that Christianity doesn't stand or fall on the way Christians behave, or have behaved throughout history. Christianity stands on the person of Jesus, who was no hypocrite.

So there we are, twelve of the most common questions that people ask about Christianity with, I trust, helpful, down-to-earth answers you can feel comfortable using. But what about questions that you don't know the answer to? Be honest, and admit that you don't have an answer, but that you'll find out and get back to them.

Please, whatever you do, don't bluff your way through an answer or even evade the question altogether, as we've all seen skilled politicians do. Make a note of the question and find the answer – from a book maybe, or a more experienced Christian – and promise to come back to the questioner. And the bonus is that you get another opportunity to spend even more time sharing your faith with them.

Finally, remember the words of Paul: '*Be wise in the way you act towards outsiders; make the most of every opportunity. Let your conversation be always full of grace, seasoned with salt, so that you may know how to answer everyone*' (Colossians 4:5–6).

Resources

One of the most effective resources in our evangelistic armoury is literature. It was one of the greatest poets of the romantic period, Lord Byron, who said, '*A drop of ink may make a million think.*' Good-quality, easy-to-read and easy-to-understand Christian literature can have a profound effect.

In 1994, Christ for all Nations (CfaN) targeted the UK for a mass mailing of the gospel booklet, *From Minus to Plus*, written by German evangelist Reinhard Bonnke. Over 70,000 people became Christians through the leaflet drop. Years later, decision cards were still received almost on a daily basis at the CfaN offices in the West Midlands. They found literature won for Jesus people who would never set foot within a church. Reinhard told one story of a woman whose husband never wanted to accept Jesus. He later died, and she grieved and grieved because she thought he didn't know Christ. A few months after his death, she found a *From Minus to Plus* booklet, and in the back of it, her husband had filled out the card indicating that he had become a Christian, even though he'd never had a chance to send it back.

Since the first launch in the UK, *From Minus to Plus* has reached into 95 million homes in twelve different countries, with tens of thousands of churches receiving converts from the resulting enquirers. The other countries targeted with the gospel booklet were Ireland, Germany, Austria, Switzerland, Liechtenstein, Norway, Denmark, Sweden, Hong Kong, Canada and the United States of America. This vision still continues actively at this present time in Finland, Greenland, Iceland and the Faroe Islands. On top of all this, Reinhard Bonnke has written a number of other books and booklets. At present, a total of over 103 million books have been translated into 123 languages and dialects, and are being printed in forty-two different countries.

A gospel booklet was key in my decision to become a Christian. As a young teenager I joined the Boys' Brigade (BB) in Bournemouth. It was a right laugh and I thoroughly enjoyed the social side of being in the BB: badge work and expeditions, camping and football. The fact that there was a Girls' Brigade was an added bonus too! But I have to say the church side was a bit of a drag – well, the one we had to go to anyway. To me as a teenager it seemed so dead it should have been buried fifty years ago. The God stuff was unintelligible to me and way above my head; that is until we went off for summer camp in Devon.

During the camp, the leaders talked about Jesus as if he were alive today, and we were all given a little booklet with a road sign on the front, called *Journey into Life*. Well, I read it, then read it again, then reread it once more for good measure, just to be absolutely sure. It was a complete revelation to me that God loved me, wanted to have a friendship with me and could change my life for the better. I decided that if it was true, then I most definitely wanted it. I thought about it all the way home on the coach and when I eventually arrived back at my house I dumped my suitcase in the kitchen, ran upstairs to my bedroom, got on my knees and prayed the prayer of commitment with all my heart. I can still remember that moment to this day. That little booklet was the catalyst for my conversion.

That's probably the main reason I use literature so much in evangelism. For years before I was a full-time evangelist, I used literature. I was forever giving tracts away, or leaving them in places where they might just get picked up. At that time I didn't feel confident enough to be able to share the gospel message with others, but I knew I could give away a book that would explain things better than I could. I could give you many stories of changed lives as a result.

These days I tend to produce my own but over the years have purchased vast quantities of tracts, booklets and Gospels that I have used to great effect. In my opinion, the best ones available today are from the Christian Publicity Organisation (CPO) in Worthing, West Sussex. I asked Steve Carroll, CPO's senior designer, for some tips on producing great literature, and some of his ideas follow.

Invitational

The aims of an invite are to establish the presence of the church in your community and provide a means of access to unbelievers. We've ascertained that most people come to Christ through friendships, so an invite is a great thing to leave with a friend, so they can pin it up, or stick it on the fridge as a permanent reminder of your church. Consider themed seasonal invitations for Christmas, Easter, harvest, etc. If the invite is to a special event then you'll probably need to include the following:

1 Name of event
2 Date
3 Time – start and finish
4 Price
5 Location
6 Map – could be useful if your venue is hard to find
7 Contact telephone number – ideally the church office
8 Description of event – we don't want to 'con' people into the kingdom. If you're planning on including some gospel explanation at the event, then say you are. I use a non-threatening phrase like 'including a short gospel presentation' or perhaps 'plus some extra special good news'.

Intriguing

The aim of intriguing literature is ultimately the creative communication of the gospel. Use images and words that will capture the imagination of the reader and make them examine Christianity for themselves. Quality counts, so invest as much as you can into good literature. I must confess to having kept copies of Hare Krishna books that were given to me on the streets. They were produced to such a high standard, I just felt I couldn't throw them away. The books were glossy, professionally bound and superbly illustrated and they remained on my bookshelves for many years.

In contrast, much of the Christian literature that I see as I'm involved with missions and one-off events is old, tatty, dated and smells musty because it's been kept in a cardboard box since the end of the Second World War. Instead of using the cheapest tracts that money can buy, why not throw them all out and invest – and it is an investment – in good-quality, glossy, up-to-date literature that is going to intrigue unbelievers and ultimately be another route through which they might be saved?

Imaginative

Dr T. J. Bach was a great missionary, and became a Christian through a piece of gospel literature. When a stranger handed him a tract on the streets of Chicago, he immediately tore it up and threw it on the pavement. Tears started running down the cheeks of the stranger. Strangely touched, Dr Bach bent down, picked up the pieces, and put them in his pocket. Returning home, he reassembled the tract, read it, and gave his life to Jesus.

Think creatively (there's that word again!) of how best to use literature. If you've spent good money on it, then giving it away willy-nilly might not be the best use of resources. Here are some ways – most of which I've personally tried – of using gospel literature:

In your home
Extend friendship to people that come to you, and it will give you a right to share what's important to you. If you have tradesmen working in your home, offer coffee, biscuits and cake. Make them feel part of the family. Have literature ready for them as well as for others who come to you, such as:

- Milkman
- Paper deliverer
- Dustbin men
- Postman – on the subject of post, you'll probably receive quantities of junk mail as we all do. Just think what might happen if all the Christians started posting back tracts in the reply-paid envelopes.
- Salespeople – either in person or on the telephone, I've said to salespeople before, 'I'll give you five minutes, if you give me five minutes.' Of course they'll want to sell you something, so nine out of ten times they will listen to you.

Out and about

Leave tracts in waiting-rooms and in any other place you think they might be read:

- Restaurants – put a tract under the tip – make sure it's a big one (the tip, not the tract!)
- Doctors
- Dentists
- Library
- Tyre and exhaust centres
- Launderette
- Barbershop
- Hairdressers
- Opticians
- Gym
- Bank
- Building societies
- Airport
- Vets
- Through people's doors.

I hope that's whetted your appetite. Anyone can give a tract away – it's the easiest thing in the world – yet the impact it can have can be staggering. I'll finish with a quote from Isaac Asimov, an author who in his lifetime penned over 500 books and knew the potential of the written word:

> If you could build a small package, something small enough to carry in your coat pocket, a machine which would instantly start and stop, in which you could instantly reverse yourself or go forward, which would require no batteries or other energy sources, and which would provide you with full information on an entire civilisation, what would you have? A book!

S-W

Social Action

An evangelist once described his mother as being love personified. As a boy he found her sitting at the dining-table with an old tramp one day. Apparently she had gone shopping, met the tramp along the way, and invited him home for dinner. During the conversation the tramp said, 'I wish there were more people like you in the world.'

Quickly his mother replied, 'Oh, there are. But you must look for them.'

The old man simply shook his head, saying. 'But I didn't need to look for you. You looked for me.'

When that mother demonstrated her Christian kindness toward the tramp she did something more than simply offer him a hot meal. It was a compassion that went out of its way to love the unlovely. And that's the story of Jesus' life, death and resurrection. He came looking for you and me in the sick, the maimed, the lame, the bruised, the broken-hearted, the homeless person, the poor and forgotten, the prisoner, the lonely and the rich. Although he was set apart, Jesus never separated himself from people and their needs. Neither did he limit himself to the spiritual part of a person; quite simply he was interested in the whole person and all of their needs.

Jesus cared for people in incredible ways. Even though he disapproved of their lifestyle, he spent time with prostitutes, eating and drinking, so that they would know that he loved and cared for them as individuals. Modern statistics tell us that the society we live in has many needs and this gives us a great opportunity to show that there is a God who cares passionately about people. The breakdown of many families has led to growing numbers of single parents, young people living on the streets and lonely senior citizens. Opportunities abound, so let's get involved and show others the love of God in action.

Love in action

I think it's fantastic that Christians are praying and campaigning on national issues, such as abortion, experimentation on human embryos and euthanasia, but I do firmly believe that social action needs to start where we are – with our friends, family, workmates and neighbours.

In the summer of 2000, thousands of young people descended upon Manchester to serve the people there. Their silent service spoke volumes about God's love and deeply impacted the city. Practical tasks involved picking up litter, clearing up graffiti, gardening, decorating and building children's playgrounds. Throughout Message 2000 they discovered that one of the most effective ways of reaching out was through action evangelism. One of the organisers, Mike Pilavachi, said:

> Message 2000 was an incredible time, but we don't want to make it a monument that we dwell on nostalgically for years to come. Instead we're seeing it as a signpost pointing us to where we think God is leading us in the future.

Perhaps mobilising 11,000 young people to affect an entire city is too ambitious for you now, but there are simple things you can do to make a difference where you live. In the village where I live, it's not unusual during the summer months to see proud homeowners mowing the grass verges outside the front of their houses. Almost all of the people in my street used to do it, apart from me and my cantankerous neighbour, George. So one day I decided to give it a go. I mowed my verge with great care, getting some really nice stripes along the grass, then to top it off, I tidied up the edges with an edging spade. Feeling very pleased with myself, I mopped my sweating brow and enjoyed a can of lager while admiring my horticultural efforts. My pristine verge certainly put poor old George's to shame. So I did his too! It probably took ten minutes, but it did wonders for our relationship and we became good friends. I hadn't realised that he was terribly lonely and miserable most of the time because his body was riddled with cancer. For the last few years of his life, George and I became quite close. And all because I decided to mow his grass verge.

Let's face it, simple actions often speak louder than words. Another time, for another neighbour, Mick, I videoed a football match. He was a huge Manchester United fan and a big match was being shown on satellite television. Mick didn't have a SKY dish but I did, so I taped it for him. Once again his reaction was wonderful and our friendship grew and blossomed. Then there was dear old Ernie, a few doors down. I just popped in to see him with our small children every so often and listened as he talked about the 'old days'. I sometimes think we got more out of these short times than he did. These tiny things proved to be deeply significant for me and my neighbours.

Good news for your community

I'm convinced that the best and most effective kind of social action is Christians responding to individuals in need: caring for the broken-hearted, feeding the hungry, clothing the naked, healing the sick and visiting those in prison. That all sounds suspiciously like something Jesus might say and do, so have a look to see the kind of impact his words had on his listeners:

> 'The Spirit of the Lord is on me, because he has anointed me to preach good news to the poor. He has sent me to proclaim freedom for the prisoners and recovery of sight for the blind, to release the oppressed, to proclaim the year of the Lord's favour.' Then he rolled up the scroll, gave it back to the attendant and sat down. The eyes of everyone in the synagogue were fastened on him, and he began by saying to them, 'Today this scripture is fulfilled in your hearing.' (Luke 4:18–21)

Once again, before you start investing in manacles to chain yourselves to the railings at the Houses of Parliament to see structures of oppression changed, don't overlook those suffering in your own area or street. I've heard a wonderful story about a Scottish church doing just that, helping others in their backyard as it were. It's a church in Edinburgh that is selling its Communion silver to 'fulfil its evangelical ministry' and help fund community projects in the area. The National Museum of Scotland is buying the seventeenth-century eighteen-piece set for £200,000 to fund work with the poor. Speaking to the *Independent on Sunday*, Associate Minister, the Rev. Mike Dawson, said: '*The silver was of no use to man or beast. Since it's a national treasure, the nation can have it. We'll use the money to help the community.*'

In another part of the UK, prostitutes operating in the red light district of Nottingham are being offered prayer, care and friendship by Youth with a Mission (YWAM) in partnership with a local church in the city. The initiative started when a team from YWAM found a prostitute operating outside the front door of their base near the church, and decided to go and pray on the street corners most used by prostitutes. Police once came across the team of young people praying at midnight and, on discovering what they were doing, drove off to tell local prostitutes that there were people praying for them. Since that time, some of the women have prayed with the team. The aim of the team is to befriend the girls, some of whom are just schoolgirls, and eventually show them that there is something better than how they are currently living.

These are just two examples of Christians demonstrating the love of God in very real ways to very needy people. People everywhere have needs. Let me challenge you to become aware of those needs nearest you and do what Jesus would do – try to meet those needs. Let's not be like the man who was telling his wife about passing a woman in a downpour of rain one afternoon. She had a puncture and was standing helpless by the side of her car. 'I thought to myself,' he said, 'how awful it is of people not to help such a poor woman. I would have stopped if

I hadn't been in such a hurry.' Let me suggest some very practical things you can do:

Adopt a granny

Have a look around your neighbourhood and consider adopting an old person who is particularly lonely or seems isolated and in need of real help. If you can't think of anyone, why not telephone an old people's home and see if there are old folk who are in particular need of companionship that you could visit on a regular basis. If you have the time and church personnel it might be appropriate to run a small service every so often with some hymns and a short talk, particularly at Christmas but perhaps at other times through the year too.

As well as listening and talking, think about practical ways you can help. That could mean shopping, gardening, collecting and returning library books, cleaning the windows, housework or painting. The list could go on and on, though don't offer things you can't deliver. Maybe plan a short trip out now and again as a special treat, and make sure you remember special occasions like birthdays, Easter, Christmas, Mothers' Day, Fathers' Day, anniversaries and the like.

Hospital visiting

Being in hospital can be a particularly upsetting time, especially for patients who get very few visitors. If you ask, your local hospital might give you permission to visit some of these especially lonely patients on a regular basis. The hospital will probably have a chapel so you might be able to get involved with running services.

Prison visiting

Jesus spoke a lot to the early Church about helping prisoners. There are many ways you can help. You could write to or even visit a prisoner and become a friend to them in that way. Our church's cricket team go into our local prison to play their cricket team. Of course that idea lends itself to most sports. I've taken books into my local prison, and on New Year's Eve 1999, the Christian prisoners delivered to the cell of every inmate a small gospel booklet that I had written, called *Millennium Man*. Hundreds of copies were very gratefully received. Most prison chaplains that I have met are overworked and under-appreciated and would welcome some help with planning services or being part of an Alpha course, so support in that way if you are able.

Gifts for the poor and needy

Social services will be aware of particularly needy families in your area. They will be able to advise on individual families and their specific needs. Imagine the impact you might have if a few of you from your church pooled some money together and bought gifts of clothes, toys and food for that family as a token of your love.

Volunteer work

This could be clearing up litter, helping to remove graffiti, tidying gardens or doing maintenance work at children's play-grounds. It could mean helping in other ways too. Most parts of the country have day centres or residential homes for those with learning difficulties and other disabilities. These are often under-staffed and most grateful for help from eager volunteers. I guarantee that you'll find this sort of social action extremely rewarding and there are loads of things that you can do to make a really positive contribution. It could be that you'll be asked to perform songs or drama, or help organise art and craft projects. You could help take the residents out to the shops, or for a walk or some other expedition, maybe even take them to a church meeting with you.

Holiday clubs

Children and teenagers often get very bored during school holidays and your church should seriously think about organising a holiday club of some sort. This could be an entire week of singing, dancing, stories, fun and games or it could be on a much smaller scale, such as organising a game of rounders or a mini football tournament over in the park. This will be a blessing to the young people and to their parents too!

I've realised I've just scratched the surface here on this subject. I've not even mentioned other vitally important social care projects such as job clubs, helping with drug and alcohol abuse, debt counselling and employment training. Those are absolutely vital as well. From experience, I've found many Christians don't get involved with social action either because they don't know where to begin, or because the problems in society seem 'just too big'. That's one reason I've suggested the ideas that I have, because they are simple things anyone can do, but will make a huge impact for Jesus and the gospel.

We've seen throughout the book that the gospel – the *good news*, really is good news for everyone. That might seem a little obvious, but it's worth saying again and again, until we really believe and start to do something about it. Real evangelism is about individual Christians and entire churches being equipped to move out into our communities to make a difference by talking about and showing the love of Jesus.

Testimony

I have to admit to being a bit of a telly addict. I avidly watch cookery shows, DIY programmes, quizzes and all the soaps, but probably most of all I love chat shows as I'm genuinely interested in other people's lives. You might put it another way, and just think I'm a bit nosy! But if we're honest I guess we all enjoy finding out what other people are like and what they're up to. The vast array of magazines with interviews and gossip proliferate the shelves of newsagents in high streets and shopping centres across the country. *Hello!* magazine, for example, continues to capture the attention of the British public, with its blend of celebrity news and pictures, as a staggering half a million copies are purchased every week. We all find other people's lives and stories just plain fascinating.

John Wesley's personal story has always made a profound impact on all who have read of it. Here is a summary of how he came to Christ. He went to Oxford Seminary in England for five years, and then became an Anglican minister for about ten years. Toward the end of this time he became a missionary from England to Georgia in the USA, in approximately 1735. All of his life he had been quite a failure in his ministry, though very devout and pious. He got up early each morning and prayed for two hours. He would then read the Bible for an hour before going to prisons and hospitals to minister to all manner of people. He would teach, pray for and help others until late at night. He did this for years. In fact, the Methodist

Church gets its name from the methodical life of piety that Wesley and his friends lived.

On the way back from America there was a huge storm at sea. The little ship in which they were sailing was about to sink. Huge waves broke over the ship and the wind roared in the sails. Wesley feared he was going to die that night and was terrified. He had no assurance of what would happen to him when he died. Despite all of his efforts to be a good man all his life, death now for him was like a big black question mark. On one side of the ship was a group of men who were singing hymns. He ran over and asked them, 'How can you sing when this very night you are going to die?'

They replied, 'If this ship goes down we will go up to be with the Lord forever.'

Wesley went away shaking his head, thinking to himself, 'How can they know that? What have they done that I haven't done?' Then he added, 'I came to convert the heathen, but who will convert me?'

Eventually the ship arrived back in England. Wesley went to London and found his way to Aldersgate Street and a small chapel. There he heard a man reading a sermon that had been written two centuries before by Martin Luther, entitled 'Luther's Preface to the Book of Romans'. This sermon described what real faith was. It was trusting Jesus for salvation, and not in good works. Wesley suddenly realised that he had been wrong all his life. That night he wrote these words in his journal:

About a quarter before nine, I felt my heart strangely warmed. I felt I did trust in Christ, Christ alone, for salvation; and an assurance was given me that He had taken away my sins, even mine, and saved me from the law of sin and death.

Following his dramatic conversion, John Wesley spent the final fifty-two years of his life riding around Britain on horseback preaching the gospel. He got up each morning at 4.00 a.m., covered 225,000 miles and preached 40,000 sermons. He said of his remarkable life and ministry, '*I look upon all the world as my parish . . . in whatever part of it I am, I judge it right to declare unto all that are willing to hear the glad tidings of salvation.'*

A personal testimony, or story, like Wesley's can have a tremendous effect on its listeners. It seems to be the case that in the Western world we have a tendency to communicate our message through stating and explaining theology. However in the East, throughout the ages, truth has mainly been communicated through storytelling. When we examine Jesus' ministry we can see that he never spoke to unbelievers without telling a story:

> Jesus spoke all these things to the crowd in parables; he did not say anything to them without using a parable. So was fulfilled what was spoken through the prophet: 'I will open my mouth in parables, I will utter things hidden since the creation of the world.' (Matthew 13:34–5)

In the same way, the early Christians didn't just tell other people about Jesus' story; they also told their own stories. Paul explained his conversion story at least twice (Acts 22 and Acts 26). Peter and John did it as well: '*For we cannot help speaking about what we have seen and heard*' (Acts 4:20). They knew, as we do today, that personal experience is a powerful witnessing tool that even the most hardened sceptic will find it hard to attack.

The problem many Christians have with sharing – or should I say, not sharing – their story is they think their story is just too normal. We've all read exciting books and heard thrilling accounts of ex-Hell's Angels, murderers, gang leaders, drug addicts and Satanists coming to know Jesus, and we feel that our story blends into insignificance because it is just too downright ordinary. Having said that, the average person in the street isn't likely to be a mass murderer or head of a witches' coven either. They're probably just pretty normal people too, so will be able to relate to your story and identify with it.

What we do need to learn to do is to make our personal story more effective. It really is possible for an 'ordinary' story to make an extraordinary impact. It's important that you take time out to plan how you communicate the way Jesus has changed you, so you can explain it in an interesting and logical way. We have already seen how Paul used his story to great effect, by dividing it into three different parts. He explained what life was like before knowing Jesus, how he came to meet him and what happened afterwards. Let's see what we can learn from his account, with fifteen tips on how to share your story more effectively:

Before

> 'Brothers and fathers, listen now to my defence.' When they heard him speak to them in Aramaic, they became very quiet. Then Paul said: 'I am a Jew, born in Tarsus of Cilicia, but brought up in this city. Under Gamaliel I was thoroughly trained in the law of our fathers and was just as zealous for God as any of you are today. I persecuted the followers of this Way to their death, arresting both men and women and throwing them into prison, as also the high priest and all the Council can testify. I even obtained letters from them to their brothers in Damascus, and went there to bring these people as prisoners to Jerusalem to be punished.' (Acts 22:1–5)

1   Tell your story as it is. It is such a temptation, particularly if we have a very ordinary story, to exaggerate our past lives a little and 'spice' the story up a bit. This is not a good idea.
2   Be yourself – chatty and interesting.
3   Be accurate – don't over emphasise how terrible you used to be, or some of the terrible things you did.
4   Be honest and explain, like Paul did:

- what you were like
- where you are from
- what life was like
- your thoughts and attitudes before you became a Christian.

5   Don't bore your listener with boring incidentals either; they probably won't really care if you were born on a Monday or a Tuesday, or whether it was raining or sunny!

During

'About noon as I came near Damascus, suddenly a bright light from heaven flashed around me. I fell to the ground and heard a voice say to me, "Saul! Saul! Why do you persecute me?" "Who are you, Lord?" I asked. "I am Jesus of Nazareth, whom you are persecuting," he replied. My companions saw the light, but they did not understand the voice of him who was speaking to me. "What shall I do, Lord?" I asked. "Get up," the Lord said, "and go into Damascus. There you will be told all that you have been assigned to do." My companions led me by the hand into Damascus, because the brilliance of the light had blinded me.

'A man named Ananias came to see me. He was a devout observer of the law and highly respected by all the Jews living there. He stood beside me and said, "Brother Saul, receive your sight!" And at that very moment I was able to see him. Then he said: "The God of our fathers has chosen you to know his will and to see the Righteous One and to hear words from his mouth. You will be his witness to all men of what you have seen and heard. And now what are you waiting for? Get up, be baptised and wash your sins away, calling on his name." ' (Acts 22:6–16)

1 Share how you realised that you had a need for Jesus in your life.
2 Explain how you became a Christian – what did you actually have to do?
3 Be simple – don't confound your listener with deep theological points.
4 Recount how you were feeling at the time of your decision and give loads of personal details
5 Remember to use language your listener can understand and relate to. Avoid all religious words and clichés. Expressions like 'saved' and 'washed in the blood' are most definitely out.

After

'When I returned to Jerusalem and was praying at the temple, I fell into a trance and saw the Lord speaking. "Quick!" he said to me. "Leave Jerusalem immediately, because they will not accept your testimony about me." "Lord," I replied, "these men know that I went from one synagogue to another to imprison and beat those who believe in you. And when the blood of your martyr Stephen was shed, I stood there giving my approval and guarding the clothes of those who were killing him." Then the Lord said to me, "Go; I will send you far away to the Gentiles." ' (Acts 22:17–21)

1 Don't be dishonest about your life after becoming a Christian. It's a fact that when people become Christians their problems don't all disappear overnight. We don't want to 'con' people into the kingdom of God.
2 Do explain how being a Christian has helped with your problems and what knowing Jesus means in your life today.
3 Be realistic – you're not what you were, but you're not completely there yet.
4 Be positive – don't knock other religions, churches or other Christians who might be a little different to you.
5 Make your story really up-to-date by changing and adding bits each week as Jesus helps you through life. Be ready to change the 'after' part of your story every week, if not every day.

I hope you can see how effective your story can be. It is worth practising in front of others and asking for constructive criticism. It could be that you want to write it down and even turn it into your own personal tract.

Personal tracts

Well-written and well-produced story tracts are very effective and could be a great resource to leave with a person you've spoken to. Christian designers and publishers like CPO in Worthing, for example, are able to produce fantastic personal tracts at very reasonable rates, though of course with the proliferation of desktop publishing packages available today, you may feel able to produce your own. Personally, I would rather pay professionals to do the job. Either way, bear in mind:

- Language – standing up and sharing your story in church on a Sunday is completely different to a written leaflet, aimed at unbelievers. I've already mentioned the need to eliminate all jargon; you also need to consider your target audience and write from their viewpoint. Try to write in a magazine style like you would read in a newspaper or popular magazine. If you don't feel able to do this well, once again, consider asking for help from someone with a good flair for words, or even perhaps a trained journalist or writer.
- Pictures – people are interested in people so try to use at least one good picture if you can. Using a picture or other suitable image will help to capture your reader's interest and visual images also stay in the mind for longer.
- Approach – as Paul did, start by painting a picture of yourself. Don't even mention God to start with. Gradually start to explain how you discovered you needed God. Explain your feelings well and your readers may well be able to identify with how you felt and realise that they might need the same help themselves.
- Honesty – honesty is the best policy, so admit your failings, though also explain that you're not what you were. Don't make out you're a super-Christian and that life's problems disappeared the moment you met Jesus. Don't exaggerate, and certainly don't adopt the tabloid maxim: 'Don't let the truth get in the way of a good story.'
- Contact details – it's good to have a contact number and address on the back, but not a good idea to put your home telephone number, for obvious reasons. Check with your church that they are happy putting their name and address and maybe even a map and details of services on the back page.

In conclusion, after you've shared your story with a person, don't just leave it at that. Why not ask: 'What do you think about having a personal relationship with Jesus yourself?' This could well be the time for a person to want it for themselves and you can lead them to Christ then and there.

In Queen Victoria's time, a beautiful young woman was invited out to dinner by William Gladstone, who was considered one of the most brilliant statesmen of the nineteenth century. On the following evening, the same young lady was escorted to a restaurant by Benjamin Disraeli, novelist, statesman and twice Prime Minister. When asked for her impression of these two rivals for her attention, she replied: 'After an evening with Gladstone, I thought he was the most brilliant man I had ever met. After an evening with Disraeli, I thought myself to be the most fascinating woman in the world!' Make your story interesting and people will be fascinated by it. So go and tell your story, and tell it as it is.

S-W

Unique

To Jesus we're all unique and special. Indeed so special that he chose to give his life upon a cross, so we might know a friendship and relationship with God. It's wonderful to look at the way Jesus looks at people as unique individuals. He doesn't only see what a person is; he also sees what they can become. He doesn't just see what the person has already done, he also sees the possibilities. The history books are full of stories of gifted persons whose talents were overlooked by a procession of people until someone believed in them. Einstein was four years old before he could speak and seven before he could read. Isaac Newton did poorly in primary school. A newspaper editor fired Walt Disney because he had 'no good ideas'. Haydn gave up ever making a musician of Beethoven, who seemed a slow and plodding young man with no apparent talent – except a belief in music. Jesus looked at Peter and saw in him not only a Galilaean fisherman but one who had it in him to become the rock on which Jesus' Church would be built. Jesus sees us not only as we are, but as we can be.

The Bible says that when a person becomes a Christian, they have been 'born again' (John 3:3). The old has gone and God has given them a fresh start, and that's where we need to play our part, because the newborn 'baby' Christian will need your help in many ways as they develop and grow in Jesus.

Because people are all unique, the way they grow in their faith will be different as it is with all children growing up and maturing at different stages. For me, my early development as a new Christian, was a slow drawn-out affair. After I had made a commitment following a Boys' Brigade camp, I was given some Bible reading notes and that was about it. I didn't really grow much for at least five years. My friend Geoff soon took me under his wing though, and visits to a lively Baptist church followed by a chat over pancakes and cups of cappuccino afterwards kept me going through the tough first few years of development. In time I found a great, lively church where I finally started to grow, at long last.

The Bible uses the word 'discipleship' for this whole process of growing in God. Jesus never once told us to go and make Christians. He was very clear:

> Then Jesus came to them and said, 'All authority in heaven and on earth has been given to me. Therefore go and make disciples of all nations, baptising them in the name of the Father and of the Son and of the Holy Spirit, and teaching them to obey everything I have commanded you.' (Matthew 28:18–20)

If you look even closer at the original text, it is probably more likely to imply: 'as you are going, as you are teaching, as you are baptising, make disciples'.

This process of disciple-making is highly important, because it's an integral part of the Great Commission. The actual word for disciple – *mathetes* – actually means learner, and comes directly from the word 'mathematics', the subject regarded by ancient scholars as the essential building block to all learning.

I guess the modern equivalent of *mathetes* would be the word 'apprentice' – someone to whom a master craftsman passes on his skills and the tricks of the trade. People often ask me how I first learned I could escape from a straitjacket. It all started when I bought some books that Houdini wrote on escaping from restraints. I quickly picked up a vast amount of theoretical information, but it wasn't until a fellow escape artist showed me, then put me in one and then taught me how to get out, that I could say I was an escape artist in my own right. In other words, head knowledge was not enough – I needed practical side-by-side instruction. As the ancient Chinese proverb goes: '*I hear – I forget, I see – I remember, I do – I understand.*'

The biblical formula goes like this:

1 The teacher works, the disciple watches him work – you learn by watching him.
2 The disciple then works with the teacher – you work together.
3 The disciple works and the teacher watches – he watches you at work.
4 The disciple becomes the teacher – you then find someone else to disciple.

It's not surprising that Jesus was the expert at this sort of thing. He was the undisputed master craftsman with a group of young apprentices. The noun *mathetes* occurs 264 times exclusively in the Gospels and the book of Acts. It was something that Jesus firmly believed in, so let's examine in more detail the model he used.

Jesus spent time

Scholars of the Bible point out that the synoptic Gospels cover only thirty-three or thirty-four days of Jesus' three-year ministry, and John records only eighteen days. So what did Jesus do the rest of the time? I believe Jesus' strategy was to concentrate his time on teaching and training his disciples, rather than speaking to large crowds. He chose to be with them and invest time with them. They were, after all, his spiritual children. As a parent, I know that the best way to raise a family is by spending time with them. In the same way, we must spend consistent, quality time with new converts, mixing social and spiritual together in a very natural way.

An important aim of discipleship is to give the new Christian an understanding of what's happened to them and a real understanding of the implications of the gospel. The parable of the sower (Matthew 13:18–23) reminds us of the dangers of lack of understanding: '*When anyone hears the message about the kingdom and does not understand it, the evil one comes and snatches away what was sown in his heart. This is the seed sown along the path'* (Matthew 13:19). We don't want to lose any converts, so carefully think through the foundations of the Christian faith that you need to teach them.

As a teacher your role is vitally important. A teacher is not there just to acquaint an individual with the tools of the trade; a teacher is a tool of the trade, no matter what that trade is. You never stop needing teachers. The great musicians never stop taking lessons, never stop trying to improve. The great concert pianist Arthur Rubinstein used to say that if he missed a day of practice, he noticed it in the quality of his performance. If he missed two days, the critics noticed. And if he missed three days, the audience noticed.

The new convert needs you to teach them the basics of growth. Teach them who they are in Christ, so they understand the process of salvation that they have recently experienced. Teach about baptism and the Holy Spirit and practically show them how to pray and get the best out of their Bible. Be honest with them. If you find Bible study and prayer a bit difficult at times – which is probably most of us – then admit your own struggles in these areas and teach them from your mistakes and show them what works for you. These things are a discipline, so why not do some of these activities together, so that you both help each other grow?

Jesus devoted his time and energy to helping others

Jesus continually gave of himself to others. Someone once said that the best things are caught and not just taught. The disciples caught his enthusiasm and heartache for the lost. Evangelism was a compulsion for Jesus, and in time his vision became their vision.

The new convert needs to be firmly rooted into a local church so they can grow. As their discipler you are vital, but the new Christian needs to receive the benefits of the wider church too. Church can be intimidating for new Christians, with unfamiliar music, vocabulary, surroundings and lots of new faces. So put yourself out as Jesus did. Don't expect the newcomer to turn up at church alone. Offer to pick them up, bring them with you and look after them. Don't leave them to sit by themselves during the meeting and drift off chatting to your friends. Stick with them, explain what's going on, involve them and introduce them to just a few of your Christian friends. Afterwards take them out to lunch, or invite them back to your house where you can take the opportunity to talk further about the meeting and answer any questions. I'll say it again: put yourself out and devote yourself to helping others.

Jesus gave them things to do

Jesus assigned his disciples jobs to do:

> When Jesus had called the Twelve together, he gave them power and authority to drive out all demons and to cure diseases, and he sent them out to preach the kingdom of God and to heal the sick. He told them: 'Take nothing for the journey – no staff, no bag, no bread, no money, no extra tunic. Whatever house you enter, stay there until you leave that town. If people do not welcome you, shake the dust off your feet when you leave their town, as a testimony against them.' So they set out and went from village to village, preaching the gospel and healing people every-where. (Luke 9:1–6)

Jesus wanted his friends to put into practice what they'd heard him say and observed him do. They had spent quality time with him and he had given himself away to them. He had prayed for them and now his plan was for these very same men to go and do the same thing themselves. This was Jesus' strategy to win the world. Of course it might not be appropriate for you to send out the new convert to the local hospital to heal all the patients – well, not in the first week anyway! It might be more appro-priate to ask them to prepare a short Bible study, or lead a small prayer group.

Help them to write out their testimony with a view to them

telling their story at a church meeting. Perhaps ask them to work on other ideas covered in this book. Pair up for a streetwork session, and after they've seen you instigating conversations with passers-by, let them take the lead. The opportunities are endless. New Christians can be the most effective witnesses – and that's a fact. They probably know more unbelievers than you do, so make the most of it.

Dr James Kennedy, founder of Evangelism Explosion, made the point that if an outstanding international evangelist was to lead 1,000 people a night to the Lord, it would take 16,348 years to reach the whole world of 6 billion people. However, if you were discipling the Jesus way, and were able to lead one person a year to the Lord and could train that person to do the same – win one other person each year – and so on, it would take just thirty-three years to win the entire planet for Jesus. Discipleship is the key.

To summarise this chapter on making better disciples, remember:

- Invest time with people
- Give yourself away
- Share your heart
- Share your vision
- Pray for them
- Take them with you
- Let them watch you at work
- Watch them at work
- Let them do the work themselves
- Give them new challenges and achievable goals.

S-W

Vision

Victor Frankl was a successful Viennese psychiatrist before he was thrown into a Nazi concentration camp. In a speech upon his release he said:

> There is only one reason why I am here today. What kept me alive was you. Others gave up hope. I dreamed. I dreamed that someday I would be here, telling you how I, Victor Frankl, had survived the Nazi concentration camps. I've never been here before, I've never seen any of you before, I've never given this speech before. But in my dreams, in my dreams, I have stood before you and said these words a thousand times.

Vision is a powerful thing – it kept Victor Frankl alive. Vision is vital in our evangelism and walk with God. If we have no vision or goals or dreams we'll continue just as we have always done and never see what God wants to see for those who don't yet know him. Vision involves seeing as God sees. We've seen through this book, time and time again, how God sees our world and people in it:

> For God so loved the world that he gave his one and only Son, that whoever believes in him shall not perish but have eternal life. For God did not send his Son into the world to condemn the world, but to save the world through him. (John 3:16–17)

That vision can and should give us a clear God-given sense of direction in our evangelism, coupled with a commitment to complete the journey in partnership with him. The mandate and instructions for the journey are simple and have remained unchanged for 2,000 years: '*Go into all the world and preach the good news to all creation. Whoever believes and is baptised will be saved, but whoever does not believe will be condemned*' (Mark 16:15–16).

God gave a man called David Hogan a vision over twenty years ago. Mississippi-born Hogan was called to work in Mexico, and specifically in the mountainous jungle area called the Yucatan, to work with two different tribes: the Aztecs and the Mayam Indians. Some twenty-two years after his initial obedience to the call of God on his life, David Hogan and his team are currently planting between nine and twelve churches a month, and on average seeing around 200 people an hour becoming Christians in that area of Mexico alone. They have also seen God break out in miraculous power and Hogan claims that there isn't a single part of the body that they haven't seen God recreate. In May 1999, while speaking in England, David Hogan explained that through their evangelistic ministry they had seen God raise 450 people from the dead. Most up-to-date reports indicate that the figure is currently in excess of 600. It's hardly any wonder that 5,000 a day are becoming Christians!

Finding vision

God wants to give vision to us. It doesn't come, necessarily, in the form of a loud, booming voice from heaven but still he speaks. Maybe through the words, advice and counsel of other Christians. It could be through a letter or telephone call, or while praying or in a time of praise and worship. It could be through the prompting of the Spirit while you're even watching television or having a bath.

When God called me to be an evangelist I was working as a steward at Spring Harvest in Minehead. A man called Philip Mohabir was preaching and at the end of his talk said that God was calling evangelists. I knew without a shadow of a doubt that God was talking directly to me that night. Upon my return home, I informed my parents (who weren't Christians) that I was leaving my well-paid banking career to become an evangelist. I soon discovered that they didn't share my enthusiasm! For months leading up to my resignation, things were hard, to say the least.

The other problem was that I was a very shy and insecure person. The thought of standing up in front of just a handful of people would so cripple me with fear that I would make myself physically sick with worry. But deep down, I knew that God had called me, and I went on to be obedient to that call and vision and have found God has used me beyond my wildest dreams.

Receiving vision

I also believe that God wants to give us vision for our friends. We started this book by looking at the story of how Ananias led Saul to the Lord. Ananias was terrified at the thought of witnessing to this persecutor of Christians so God showed Ananias a vision of how he would use Saul if he became a Christian: '*Go! This man is my chosen instrument to carry my name before the Gentiles and their kings and before the people of Israel. I will show him how much he must suffer for my name*' (Acts 9:15–16). If you're struggling for breakthrough in your witnessing, ask God for a vision of how he might use the person in question, if they became a Christian. Start to see 'God potential' in people – it really does work.

At one time Andrew Carnegie was the wealthiest man in North America. He went there from his native Scotland when he was a small boy, did a variety of odd jobs, and eventually ended up as the largest steel manufacturer in the United States. At one time he had forty-three millionaires working for him. In those days a millionaire was a rare person; conservatively speaking, a million dollars in his day would be equivalent to at least £15,000,000 today. A reporter asked Carnegie how he had hired forty-three millionaires. Carnegie responded that those men had not been millionaires when they started working for him but had become millionaires as a result.

The reporter's next question was, 'How did you develop these men to become so valuable to you that you have paid them this much money?' Carnegie replied that men are developed the same way gold is mined. When gold is mined, several tons of dirt must be moved to get an ounce of gold; but one doesn't go into the mine looking for dirt – one goes in looking for the gold.

In the same way, let's not look for the flaws and blemishes in people. Humanly speaking our friends or relatives might seem a million miles away from God and becoming a Christian. So instead look for the gold, not for the dirt; the good, not the bad. Look for the positive aspects of their lives. See them as God sees them.

Focusing vision

One of the world's most successful fast-food companies is Domino's Pizza. They are a wonderful, and I might add very tasty, example of a top company that has a very clearly defined vision. Their strategy is very focused. In the words of their founder, '*Domino's has a single goal. Its mission is simple: to deliver a high-quality pizza, hot, within thirty minutes at a fair price.*' Everything they do at Domino's is centred on that goal.

In the same way, I firmly believe we need to focus, plan and strategise our evangelism. Of course we always need to be open to the prompting and direction of the Holy Spirit, but I personally feel that the attitude of 'Let's leave it to the Lord and it'll all work out' is sometimes just an excuse for people to be lazy and do nothing significant about reaching the lost.

God is a strategist. The entire Bible, from cover to cover, reflects God's strategy. From the very start of the Old Testament we see God's strategy worked out through people like Noah, Abraham, Joseph and David. They provided a backdrop for what was to come through Jesus. God had a plan, and his timing was perfect. Jesus came not just by accident – when God felt like it – but at a key moment in human history. Two thousand years ago, Roman government was reasonably stable, the road system made travel easier, and a common language, Greek, made communication better.

In Matthew's Gospel we read of Jesus' strategy. *'Jesus went through all the towns and villages, teaching in their synagogues, preaching the good news of the kingdom and healing every disease and sickness'* (Matthew 9:35). His strategy was to start in the small towns and villages, working his way towards Jerusalem. The well-known Jewish historian, Josephus, states in his histories that Jesus' goal was to reach around 15,000 people in 204 villages. There is no doubt about it; God had a specific strategy in mind and he put it into action through his beloved Son, Jesus, who came to save the world.

These were Jesus' words to his disciples before he ascended into heaven: *'But you will receive power when the Holy Spirit comes on you; and you will be my witnesses in Jerusalem, and in all Judea and Samaria, and to the ends of the earth'* (Acts 1:8). Here Jesus was sharing his fourfold vision and strategy for worldwide evangelisation. Let's take a closer look at the implications behind his final instructions:

Jerusalem – local

For the disciples Jerusalem was their local city, with a population of around 50,000. It was the place where they lived and worked and also the place where they had made the most mistakes. For us too, this could well be the hardest place to evangelise. This is the place where people know you and know what you're really like! Your Jerusalem would probably include the place that you work, your immediate family and of course neighbours.

Judea – national

Judea was the name of the large territory ruled by Herod the Great. It was the wider area outside Jerusalem. The culture and language would have been the same, but it was a bigger, arid, mountainous area. Our Judea is likely to be people that we see from time to time. Perhaps we hear from them only once or twice a year at Christmas or around birthdays. These people may be colleagues from offices outside our immediate area that we know and have friendships with. Start thinking of neighbours who have moved away, or friends who have gone to universities in other parts of the country, or workmates who have been transferred to other branches.

Distant relatives could fall into this category and if you start to jot names down you will probably end up with quite a list. How about putting this book down this very minute, and giving them a call to say 'hello'? Or write a note, or send an e-mail to maintain the contact and keep the relationship going. These are people you need to reach.

Samaria – cross-cultural

Samaria was built on a hill rising some 300 feet above the surrounding plain. In Jesus' day the Samaritans regarded themselves as part of Israel, but the Jews wanted nothing to do with the Samaritans, partly because it was the ancestors of the Samaritans who had opposed the rebuilding of Jerusalem. The Jews tried to avoid travelling through Samaria, and a Jew would not sit down to eat with a Samaritan. At times, Samaritans were regarded as worse and more ungodly than Gentiles (John 8:48).

Start to think about who you might not choose to talk to and spend time with and this will be your Samaria. If you're the managing director of an international company, then it could be the office cleaner and vice versa. It could be the neighbour at number 38 whose dog always manages to relieve itself on your grass verge! Then again, it might just be the down-and-out who sits at the bus stop drinking special brew from dawn to dusk. If you're still a student and in the sixth form at school, for example, the kids in the first year, who you just refuse to even acknowledge, might be your Samaria. For me, it was my neighbour June, who I once called a 'stupid woman' (I know, it's terrible, isn't it?), and then felt I had to apologise to her and buy a small gift. Going to Samaria will make other people sit up and take notice, because it's not normal – so go and do it.

Ends of the earth – international

The ends of the earth have no limits whatsoever. With opportunities in world travel, I guess there's probably not one single country on earth that you couldn't be in within around 36 hours. One of the highlights of my years of ministry was preaching the gospel at a squatter camp in one of the most dangerous cities in the world, Johannesburg. Standing on the back of an old pick-up truck and sharing the gospel with a sea of black faces hanging on to my every word, I was reminded of the words of the great missionary, C. T. Studd: '*Some wish to live within the sound of church and chapel bell. I wish to run a rescue mission within a yard of hell.*' That day, among the poverty and violence, large numbers of men, women, boys and girls met the Lord Jesus for themselves. It was awesome.

There's something about going to other countries and cultures that stirs faith and makes you change for good. Before his untimely death in a tragic plane accident in July 1982, American musician and evangelist Keith Green would challenge people by asking: '*We should not be asking ourselves the question "Should we go?" The question is "Is God telling me to stay?"*' If it's just impossible for you to go right now, why not invest money in others who are able? How about adopting a missionary and investing money into their ministry? Your regular support could make all the difference.

Let me inspire you with a quote from David Livingstone, who wrote in his journal on one occasion concerning his 'selfless' missionary life:

People talk of the sacrifice I have made in spending so much of my life in Africa. Can that be called a sacrifice which is simply paying back a small part of the great debt owing to our God, which we can never repay? Is that a sacrifice which brings its own blest reward in healthful activity, the consciousness of doing good, peace of mind and a bright hope of glorious destiny hereafter? Away with the word in such a view and with such a thought! It is emphatically no sacrifice. Say rather it is a privilege.

Sharing your faith is a privilege.

Using vision

A survey was taken recently of people who were over ninety-five years old. The people were asked one, open-ended question they could answer any way they wished. The question was: If you could live your life over again, what would you do differently? Among all the different answers, these three answers came back most frequently:

1 If I could live my life over again, I would reflect more.
2 If I could live my life over again, I would risk more.
3 If I could live my life over again, I would do more things that would live on after I'm dead.

If God has given you a vision then you need to work to make it happen. Determination is essential. James, the brother of Jesus made things crystal clear:

> Now listen, you who say, 'Today or tomorrow we will go to this or that city, spend a year there, carry on business and make money.' Why, you do not even know what will happen tomorrow. What is your life? You are a mist that appears for a little while and then vanishes. Instead, you ought to say, 'If it is the Lord's will, we will live and do this or that.' As it is, you boast and brag. All such boasting is evil. Anyone, then, who knows the good he ought to do and doesn't do it, sins. (James 4:13–17)

Having vision isn't easy. But ultimately we need to get on and do it, whatever the cost. Visionaries tend to be misunderstood. They struggle with doubt on occasions and can face opposition from sometimes the strangest of places; from family, friends and even Christians. Vision costs in terms of time and money. But visionaries are determined. I love the story of Jackie Pullinger who was rejected as being unsuitable for missionary life in the Far East. She knew God had planted a vision in her heart, so she went to Hong Kong by herself, and God blessed her in awesome ways.

There's a lot of other things I could say about using vision, but I really don't think I could express them any better, or even half as well for that matter, as American preacher and sociologist, Tony Campolo who said:

> It is true that there are great possibilities for failure when taking risks. And, if you fail, there are people who will mock you. But mockers are not important. Those who like to point out when the risk-takers stumble, don't count. The criticisms of those who sit back, observe and offer smug suggestions can be discounted. The promised land belongs to the person who takes the risks, whose face is marred with dust and sweat, who strives valiantly while daring everything, who may err and fall, but who has done his or her best. This person's place shall never be with those cold and timid souls who know neither victory nor defeat. Oh, if only I could persuade timid souls I meet to listen to that inner voice of the Spirit, which challenges us to attempt great things for God and expect great things from God.

In conclusion, vision comes from God and can become a reality when you start to do something about it. Ask God for vision for your life and vision for what he has in mind for others. Share other people's vision too and let's go forward with God to make a difference. Allow me to leave you with the words of a wonderful old hymn by Mary Elizabeth Byrne and Eleanor Henrietta Hull.

> Be thou my vision, O Lord of my heart,
> Be all else but nought to me, save that thou art;
> Be thou my best thought in the day and the night
> Both waking and sleeping, thy presence my light.
>
> Be thou my wisdom, be thou my true word,
> Be thou ever with me, and I with thee, Lord;

Be thou my great Father, and I thy true son;
Be thou in me dwelling, and I with thee one.

Be thou my breastplate, my sword for the fight;
Be thou my whole armour, be thou my true might;
Be thou my soul's shelter, be thou my strong tower:
O raise thou me heavenward, great power of my power.

Riches I need not, nor man's empty praise:
Be thou mine inheritance now and always;
Be thou and thou only the first in my heart:
O Sovereign of heaven, my treasure thou art.

High King of heaven, thou heaven's bright sun,
O grant me its joys after victory is won;
Great heart of my own heart, whatever befall,
Still be thou my vision, O ruler of all.

World Wide Web

The World Wide Web (WWW) has massive potential for evangelism. It was Bill Gates of Microsoft who said: '*The Internet is the first medium that distributes information globally at almost no cost.*' We've examined what Jesus said about *'going into all the world'* – I believe the Internet could be one way of fulfilling that commission to great effect – if we choose to get involved. Trust me, it's easier than you think and your involvement could make a profound difference to people's lives.

It could well be that your church has a web site already, but a church web site isn't necessarily an evangelistic web site. There's often a huge difference between the two. Of course your congregation will be interested in photos of your minister and details of whose turn it is to prepare the flowers next Sunday, but is unlikely to hold the interest of someone who's not a Christian and maybe has found your site by accident. Using your site as an electronic newsletter is fine, but we need to see the bigger picture if we're going to use the Internet to its full potential in the third millennium.

We do need to think beyond communicating church information. That could mean that you need to consider developing another site, which is purely evangelistic – which of course can be linked from your regular church site. Just think of the impact it could have. Having church information on the WWW is fine for updating your congregation, but it is unlikely that an unbeliever will just stumble across it unless they're specifically looking for it. Youth for Christ (YFC) now employ a full-time

Internet worker after discovering that 70 per cent of sixteen- to twenty-five-year olds use the Internet regularly.

Tony Whittaker, an Internet expert, was interviewed in *Idea* magazine upon his return from an Internet evangelism conference in Florida. He has estimated that out of approximately 30,000 English language Christian sites, less than 1 per cent are even broadly evangelistic. Unfortunately, this isn't surprising. He said: '*Go into any Christian bookshop. Ninety-nine per cent of the titles and videos are designed for a Christian audience.*' To reach the unreached, as we've seen throughout this book, we need to connect, engage and talk the same language. The same is true for a web site.

Being virtually computer illiterate myself, I realise I'm getting out of my depth as I'm writing this chapter! It sometimes takes me half a day to read my e-mails, let alone do something complicated like open an attachment, so I'm indebted to Jill Troup who has given me permission to reproduce a large chunk of her article that appeared in *Idea* magazine (January/February 2001) on 'Cyber E-vangelism'. The article suggested a number of ideas and tips for creating a good evangelistic web site, to which I've added some of my own thoughts:

Goals

Who do you want to visit your site? Aiming for one specific group will probably be more successful than hoping to hit everyone. Consider your target audience. It might be children, teenagers or adults. You might wish to specifically target men or women, backslidden Christians, or even Bikers as my friend Paul Sinclair – the Faster Pastor – does to great effect.

Focus

Do you want your site to be overtly Christian and evangelistic or do you want to take a step back and attract those interested in finding out about spirituality in general, and lead them towards the Christian faith? You can create a site on almost anything, and weave in the spiritual content as you choose. Some ideas are:

- Community site – an information-packed site on your town, which contains the best secular links for leisure, eating out, schools, travel, plus churches and gospel content.
- Famous site – if you live in an area that's already well-known for something – a historic building, for example – capitalise on it by creating a useful site about the attraction and area. Of course, include Christian links.
- Events site – this would be an on-line calendar of future evangelistic events for all ages, that your church is arranging, that would be suitable for unbelievers to attend.
- Youth site – this could be written by your church's teenagers for their own peer group, with links to appropriate church events for youth and to other Christian teen sites. I mentioned earlier that Youth for Christ employs a full-time Internet youth worker. The YFC site offers chat rooms, music and the Christian message in teenspeak. '*We found there was a void between the interest kids showed in the gospel and discipleship. Now when we've done a mission in one area, kids log on, usually to get the music,*' said Richard Bromley of YFC. '*They can interact with our Internet worker, who is linked with YFC mission teams, and they can get in on a discussion group.*' YFC have found that around forty hours are spent on line before someone wants a personal contact. They eventually plan to link those contacts to one of the 400 YFC-connected churches.
- Magazine site – we have already talked about the power of a good story, told well, and the impact that it can have upon its listener. Consider producing a virtual magazine with news, views, handy hints, book and movie reviews, which is also packed with testimonies to show what God has done in people's lives.
- Sermons and talks – I wouldn't use the word 'sermon' on the site itself, but essentially this site would include the text of recent talks and preaches – particularly those with an evangelistic edge. I think this could have tremendous potential for genuine seekers who wish to examine the claims of Christianity in a totally anonymous and non-threatening way.
- Books and resources – how about offering direct links to sites that offer high-quality Christian books, tapes and videos?

A good site would review books, make suggestions for recommended reading, and would have an easily understandable shopping-cart procedure for actually purchasing the books on line.

- Problem page – many people turn to the Church for answers to problems or during a crisis in life. This sort of site could offer answers to common problems, and perhaps specific pastoral help through e-mail or even personal contact.
- Prayer site – we know that prayer works, I've said that time and time again throughout this book. Wouldn't it be awesome if you were able to have a site in which people could make prayer requests? Your prayer team would then pray for the situation. Just imagine the sort of impact that could have when prayers are answered on a consistent basis.
- Spirituality – a site to explore life's big questions and issues of faith and spirituality, once again, in a non-threatening way.

Design

An evangelistic web site is essentially an advert for Christianity, so it needs to be of a high quality. Unfortunately, your church might not have an expert web designer in the congregation, or for that matter the budget to create and maintain your own web site. If this is the case, the answer might be to club together with other churches in your area or denomination, and get a professional to do it for you.

At the time of writing (May 2001) I'm told that for professional web design you would expect to pay a minimum of £50 per hour, and sometimes considerably more. If you choose to go this route, why not ask to sit in with the designer and learn from them. You could ask them to set up a template, which you then use yourself to fill in details. A lot can be achieved without necessarily buying a state-of-the-art, all-singing, all-dancing, all-praising site. The most successful sites stick to the adage of 'less is more', so keep it simple.

Maintenance

Creating the site is just the beginning; maintaining the site takes time and commitment. If your site is to contain time-sensitive information – for example, an events diary – it will need regular updating. Develop it at a level you can sustain. The job of site maintenance could well be the opportunity for someone in your church, who might not feel they have a role elsewhere, to own and run with. For a retired, disabled or unemployed person or for someone who is too scared to do other evangelism, this could be their opportunity to shine.

Links

With some excellent sites already on line, there's no need to reinvent the wheel. Using the best of what's already out there – by linking your site to them – would immediately increase the evangelistic potential of your own site. Always consider your site from a non-Christian's point of view, and create links that allow for intuitive navigation around the site for them. Most importantly, keep checking that the links are still working.

Hits

Your web site stands or falls on how easily it can be found. You might have designed the best Christian site in the history of Christendom, but if no one ever visits it, then it's a waste of time, effort and money. Finding your site depends on how and where you list it. You need to keep working at getting listed on some of the biggest and most popular search engines.

Publicity

Don't forget to include your web site address on all publicity materials, Gospels, tracts, church leaflets, notice-board, etc. An easily registered domain name, minus a string of backslashes and hyphens will be easy to remember and will help potential visitors. Also, think creatively about publicity. One south London church that backs onto a mainline railway has a huge banner on its rooftop which reads 'go surfing this Sunday', with the church's web site details.

In conclusion let me say this. For far too long the Church has remained either behind-the-times, or too eager to complain about the dangers of modern technology. According to a report published in May 2001, four out of ten homes in Britain have access to the Internet. The research group NetValue has estimated that 12.8 million people are now regular Internet users in the UK. Those figures are staggering, so let's not miss the boat on this one.

Xmas

Many years ago the land of Persia was ruled by a wise and much loved shah who cared greatly for his people and wanted only what was best for them. One day he disguised himself as a poor man and went to visit the public baths. The water for the baths was heated by a furnace in the cellar, so the shah made his way to the bowels of the building to sit with the man who was in charge of the fire. The two men shared a meagre meal, and they became friends. Day after day the ruler came to visit the man.

Eventually the shah revealed his true identity, and he expected the man to ask for him for money or a gift. Instead he looked long into his leader's face and with love and wonder in his voice said, 'You left your palace and your glory to sit with me in this dark place, to eat my coarse food, and to care about what happens to me. On others you bestow riches and gifts, but to me you have given yourself.'

Apparently that's a true story, and it wonderfully illustrates what happened that first Christmas, when God left heaven and came to earth as a man in the form of Jesus. Let me also offer a word of explanation to those offended by the spelling of Christmas, taking 'Christ out of Christmas' and all that. Let me say two things in my defence. First, of course 'Xmas' is the colloquial, with 'X' for the initial *'chi'*, the twenty-second letter of the Greek alphabet meaning *Khristos*, or Christ. And second, it's pretty hard finding words beginning with 'X'! So I hope you forgive me.

Grovelling apologies and the Greek lesson aside, I do have a sneaking suspicion that God actually likes Christmas. Not the over-indulgence, greed, jealousy, mounting credit card bills or selfishness that can easily permeate the Christmas season, but instead he likes the sense of occasion, togetherness and celebration. After all, Jesus came to give life, in all its fullness, and Christmas is a fantastic opportunity to share about this life as we communicate the gospel to a fertile audience that are ready and open to listen.

You might have expected the Son of Almighty God to have been born in a palace or a huge mansion, but he ended up coming into the world in a smelly little stable in a tiny town stuck in the middle of nowhere. Even the bustling crowds in Bethlehem at that time didn't have an inkling that the Son of God was asleep in their little town. Indeed, at his actual birth, only a few simple shepherds came to see him, yet they left different people, glorifying God, because the Saviour had been born. A statement was being made here; Jesus had come for ordinary people.

His birth occurred of course on 25 December AD 1 . . . or did it? Well, it might seem a bit daft, considering this was one of the most monumental moments in the whole history of the world, but we don't really know exactly when he was born. In fact, even the precise year is uncertain. It certainly wasn't in the year AD 1 as the calendar's *Anno Domini* (Year of the Lord) suggests.

The thing is, our dating system derived from an error about the year of Jesus' birth, made by a sixth-century monk in Rome, Dionysius Exigus, in working out the starting point of the Christian era. Scholars since have calculated that Jesus' birth happened about 5 or 7 BC (which of course rather ironically means 'Before Christ'). The revised time was determined partly by the fact that Herod the Great ruled Judea when Jesus was born and the history books record that Herod died in March, 4 BC.

As to what month the birth occurred, or on what day, that has been a matter of great speculation for many centuries. Possible dates include: 6 January, 2 February, 25 March, 19 April,

20 May, 4 October and 17 November. We do know for sure it certainly wasn't 25 December. A British physicist and astronomer David Hughes calculated that the date was 17 September, 7 BC, based on various scientific evidence, including that of a conjunction of two planets, Jupiter and Saturn, in the constellation of Pisces on that date. He concludes in a book that this extraordinary celestial display was the '*star*' seen by the distant wise men. The seventeenth-century German astronomer Johannes Kepler similarly had calculated a three-planet conjunction, including Venus as well as Jupiter and Saturn, in the same constellation in 7 BC.

Most scholars would now accept that Jesus was probably born around the middle of September in 5 BC, so what is the reason for our celebrations being based around 25 December? Well, until the fourth century, 25 December was a pagan feast day to celebrate the power of the '*sun*'. Then Constantine, the Roman emperor at the time, became a Christian and decided to turn that day into a feast day to celebrate the birth of the '*Son*' of God.

But for all the clouded chronology and background of that first Christmas, one fact is clear – God entered the world as part of it and in love with it. American rock-singer Joan Osborne's song 'One of Us' was in the charts in 1996 for weeks, with some interesting lyrics. '*What if God was one of us? Just a slob like one of us.*' I'm sure some religious people were offended by the insinuation that God was a slob. But I like the song and its sentiments. For God chose to come to earth as a human being, indeed a tiny baby who was born in a stinking stable next door to a pub. And of course that's what Christmas is all about. It's not about turkey, tinsel and toffees! No, it's that God left the splendour of heaven and came in flesh and blood to live with us for a while to make a difference.

So we've seen that Jesus wasn't actually born on 25 December, but that is the time when our family, friends and neighbours celebrate it and is the time that we, as a Church, are *expected* to celebrate it. It's also the time we're expected to communicate our faith in Jesus. In a MORI (Market and Opinion Research International) Poll, that appeared in the *Mail on Sunday*

(17 December 2000), 72 per cent of those asked understood the term 'nativity' was to do with the story of Christ's birth, and a staggering 37 per cent of adults expected to go to church at Christmas, so make the most of it.

Don't explain, of course, that Jesus wasn't actually born at the end of December – don't be a show-off. Christmas is a time of opportunities, when friends, family, colleagues and neighbours will ask: 'What are you doing for Christmas?' So let's not disappoint them. Here are some ideas to make your next Christmas a real cracker!

Toy service

A special service hosted and run by the children's groups in your church. Ask the children to all bring a small toy (with a maximum price, say £2.50), wrapped and marked – either for a boy or a girl – to be distributed over the Christmas period to children in need.

Pantomime

You might not have any Australian soap stars or ex-Gladiators in your church, but you could still put on a decent pantomime. This of course will be a well-rehearsed, good-quality affair. It may not be the time to present the gospel, but instead a time to laugh and fellowship together. If the audience enjoyed the show, then it would certainly be a great time to invite them to a more high-profile Christmas evangelistic event.

Senior citizens' meal

Invite the older folk from your area to a free, three-course, slap-up Christmas meal, followed by some entertainment from the young people in your church. The older folk will be blessed to bits by some songs and carols from the children. You might even feel brave enough to unleash a performance of the afore-mentioned pantomime on them!

Food for thought

You also could invite adults to a nice dinner. Once again quality is so important, so prepare and serve the best menu you can possibly afford. Create a cosy ambience with nice table decorations, decent tablecloths and candles. Book a really good after-dinner speaker who can share a Christmas gospel message. Afterwards serve coffee and mince pies, so people stay a little longer and can chat over what's been said.

Carol-singing

Christmas carols have been merrily sung for the last 500 years, so why not do carol-singing with a difference? As I've suggested before, instead of collecting money, why not give your listeners a gift? It could be a mince pie, or a small booklet that unwraps the true meaning of Christmas. If you do choose to collect money, make it very clear you're collecting for a charity, to bless others.

Carol service

People expect to hear about Jesus at a carol service, so let's do a really decent job of presenting him in a way that is understood, packaged around familiar hymns and carols. Serve mince pies and mulled wine afterwards, but most of all give your audience an opportunity to respond to the gospel message.

Social action

There are loads of things you can do that will bless others and demonstrate the love of Jesus to them at Christmas. Have a think and you'll come up with lots of practical things to be done. Here are just six examples:

1 Offer support to a prisoner – be a friend to a prisoner or help their family, perhaps by sending a small gift.
2 Shopping – take the housebound out shopping. If they can't

manage that, then do their shopping for them.

3　Housework – we all know how much there is to be done around the holiday period, so why not offer to address and post Christmas cards for those who aren't able to do it? You could offer to put the tree and other decorations up for an elderly or disabled person.

4　Visitation – deliver a mince pie and a Christmas card to those who live alone.

5　Meals – cook meals or even arrange a Christmas dinner for the homeless.

6　Volunteer to help man a helpline – for the Samaritans, for example.

Greetings cards

Christmas cards were used only by the wealthy 150 years ago. These days the Royal Mail tells us that in the UK we send 1.6 billion Christmas cards every year. That's a staggering amount. Every year most of us send Christmas cards to most of the people we know, but often the message is just 'Have a Merry Christmas'. I think maybe we are missing the opportunity to say more.

Last Christmas I published my own Christmas card, complete with envelope, but also with added punch. For it also contained a full-colour gospel booklet that unwrapped the true meaning of Christmas. Now you might not feel able to produce your own card, but you could slip a nice Christmassy tract inside – that would be a very easy thing to do.

In conclusion, make the most of Christmas. Many Christians seem to be so negative about Christmas and the celebrations that accompany the season. They moan and complain about this, that and the other and even see red (no pun intended) with talk of dear old Santa. If that's you, then stop being such a killjoy and instead learn to turn these things around, take full advantage of the wonderment of Christmas and introduce people to Jesus – the greatest gift known to humankind.

X-Z

Yakka

Lovers of all things antipodean, will instantly know what *Yakka* means. For those of you who wouldn't know the difference between *Neighbours* and *Home and Away*, let me explain that *Yakka* is Australian slang for 'work' – something that we all spend a considerable part of our lives doing. If you're a student, your work will be school, college or university so there's no cop-out for you, as most of the principles in this penultimate chapter should apply to you too.

Let me start by telling you what happened to me one day at work during a lunch break. It was my first week at a new branch of the bank where I worked, after leaving school as a fresh-faced sixteen-year-old. I was sitting in the staffroom, minding my own business, with another twenty of my banking colleagues, when a question came from the head cashier, a woman who for some inexplicable reason had taken an instant dislike to me the minute I'd walked in the door. During a lull in the general lunch-time chit-chat, she looked at me with disdain and asked in a loud voice, so everyone would hear, 'So how long have you been a Jesus freak?' The room fell silent and I was completely taken aback.

In retrospect, this could have been the opportunity I had been praying for – to explain to all my work colleagues that knowing Jesus wasn't an abnormal thing, but the most natural thing in the world. I could have shared how Jesus had changed my life and given me a fresh purpose for living. But instead, nothing came to mind. My mouth dried up, I went as red as a lobster, I spilled my coffee down the front of my new suit and just about managed to mumble, 'Oh, um . . . just a few years I suppose.' It all went quiet for a few moments and then the conversation moved back onto what had happened on last night's edition of *Coronation Street*. My evangelistic ministry at work did gradually improve I'm pleased to say, and I even became great friends with the head cashier!

The workplace is a great place to do evangelism; after all Jesus said we should. Now of course he didn't specifically command us to 'work for Barclays Bank because of the great opportunities for preaching the gospel'. What Jesus actually said was: '*Go into all the world and preach the good news to all creation*' (Mark 16:15). Like it or not, the *world* includes your place of work.

No, of course you're not to get silly about it and go at it non-stop. If you work in a bank like I did, please don't substitute bank notes with copies of *Journey into Life* in the cash machines, or pin crosses on staff notice-boards, or even think about giving out gospel materials every time someone cashes a cheque. That would be plain stupid and, after all, you are at work to work, and not to be the next Billy Graham. However, our witness at work is very important and there are a number of things you can do to make it more effective:

Be kind

Go out of your way to be kind and considerate, though I have a confession to make. I fell out with my office manager at work who had given me a bad report once for not taking my job seriously enough. I was determined to get revenge, so I got the poor man on every possible mailing list I could find. For months I used to love watching him open the mail at the office, and seeing his face as he opened post from Saga holidays for pensioners, Stanna stair-lifts and a whole host of companies offering surgical supports for the infirm. Awful, I know, so don't do what I did in a moment of madness!

I hope this doesn't sound too super-spiritual, but the way we treat our workmate is the way we treat God. You might be the only example of a 'real' Christian your colleagues ever see. In a crazy commercial world of dog-eat-dog, people tend to have little time for each other – so make time. Help others and go out of your way to remember birthdays and other special occasions. Take an interest in your colleagues' lives outside work and take a genuine interest in their problems.

I was reminded of the importance of this principle while reading a Winnie the Pooh story to my two-year-old daughter, Emmie. Let me share it with you, so I hope you're sitting comfortably:

> One day Pooh Bear is about to go for a walk in the Hundred Acre wood. It's about eleven-thirty in the morning. It is a fine time to go out to visit his friends – just before lunch. So Pooh sets out across the stream, stepping on the stones, and when he gets right in the middle of the stream he sits down on a warm stone and thinks about who would be the best person to visit. He says to himself, 'I think I'll go see Tigger.' No, he dismisses that. Then he says, 'Owl!' Then, 'No, Owl uses big words, hard-to-understand words.' At last he cheers up! 'I know! I think I'll go see Rabbit. I like Rabbit. Rabbit uses encouraging words like, "How's about lunch?" and "Help yourself, Pooh!" Yes, I think I'll go see Rabbit.'

It's been said that kindness has converted more sinners than either zeal, eloquence or learning. It's true, let others be astonished at your kindness and be ready to explain why, because they're bound to ask sooner or later.

Be honest

According to a survey of 800 directors, managers and partners published in *Management Today* in 2001, more than two in three believe everyone lies to their boss. The findings go on to suggest that *'unethical behaviour is endemic in the workplace'*. William Shakespeare, who knew a thing or two, said these words: *'No legacy is so rich as honesty.'* It might well be the case that everyone in your office fiddles travelling expenses, fills out time sheets incorrectly, surfs the net, makes endless private telephone calls and pilfers copious amounts of paper, pens, ruler, erasers and sellotape from the stationery cupboard to take home. Just because 'everyone does it' doesn't mean you should. Be honest, keep your promises and your colleagues will trust you.

I'm reminded of the following story about a woman who was holidaying on a beach on the south coast of England. A small boy in his swimming trunks, carrying a towel, came up to her and asked her, 'Do you believe in God?'

She was surprised by the question but replied, 'Why, yes, I do.'

Then he asked her: 'Do you go to church every Sunday?'

Again, her answer was 'Yes!'

Then he asked: 'Do you read your Bible and pray every day?'

Again she said, 'Yes!' But by now her curiosity was very much aroused.

At last the lad sighed and said, with obvious relief, 'Will you hold my wallet while I go in swimming?'

Take a stand for absolute honesty right from the start – the results could be very interesting.

Be ready

Former American President Abraham Lincoln said: '*I'll study and get ready and be prepared for my opportunity when it comes.*' Those are very wise words. You're not at work to Bible-bash people or to preach at them, but instead to be ready and prepared to give an account for your faith: '*Be wise in the way you act towards outsiders; make the most of every opportunity. Let your conversation be always full of grace, seasoned with salt, so that you may know how to answer everyone*' (Colossians 4:5–6).

I remember once after work, my mate Kevin and I went to the gym. After a good work-out, we were sitting in the Jacuzzi when out-of-the-blue he asked: '*How long have you been a born-again Christian?*' Now, that's not a bad opening question is it? Kev started coming to church soon after, and he was just one of a handful from the bank who came along with me. So be ready, even when you least expect it. The opportunity could be with the lowliest office junior or the most senior executive. Whatever they might think of their status, in the eyes of God they're exactly the same. This could also be a useful point to remember, next time you pluck up the courage to ask for time off or a raise!

Be different

You can choose your friends but you can't choose your family. The same could be said about your workmates. You'll probably have very little say in whom you are thrown together to work with. As well as having different beliefs, they'll have different values, morals and language to you, as well as some extremely irritating habits. But the fact is, you might end up spending more time with these strangers than you will with your spouse or friends, perhaps even forty to fifty hours every week for forty-eight weeks of the year. You'll get to know them well, and they'll see the real you.

I mentioned earlier how I worked for a bank straight after leaving school. A lot of my colleagues who soon became good friends could never figure me out. I was 'one of the lads' and enjoyed a pint or two, but didn't get drunk. I would go to parties and out nightclubbing with them, but didn't chat up all the women and sleep around. I'd have a laugh at the office, but wouldn't gossip behind other people's backs. This intrigued them and they used to ask why I was so different, and of course it gave me an open door of opportunity to explain why. In the workplace, this seems to me to be the best way of doing evangelism. It was Mark Twain who said: '*Always do right. This will surprise some people and astonish the rest.*' Your witness will speak volumes. – so be a good one.

I'm going to leave the last words with Mother Theresa of Calcutta who died in the latter part of the twentieth century. Although it's unlikely you'll be working with the poor and dying in the slums of India, catch the heart of what she's saying. Your colleagues might not be 'poor' in the material sense, but if they don't know Jesus they'll most definitely be 'poor in spirit'. See how you can apply these words of Mother Teresa to your friends in your workplace:

I'm still convinced that it is he and not I. That's why I was not afraid; I knew that if the work was mine it would die with me. But I knew it was his work, that it will live and bring much good. If the work is looked at just by our own eyes and only from our own way, naturally, we ourselves can do nothing. But in Christ we can do all things. That's why this work has become possible, because we are convinced that it is he, he who is working with us and through us in the poor and for the poor.

Zacchaeus

Jesus entered Jericho and was passing through. A man was there by the name of Zacchaeus; he was a chief tax collector and was wealthy. He wanted to see who Jesus was, but being a short man he could not, because of the crowd. So he ran ahead and climbed a sycamore-fig tree to see him, since Jesus was coming that way.

When Jesus reached the spot, he looked up and said to him, 'Zacchaeus, come down immediately. I must stay at your house today.' So he came down at once and welcomed him gladly.

All the people saw this and began to mutter, 'He has gone to be the guest of a "sinner".'

But Zacchaeus stood up and said to the Lord, 'Look, Lord! Here and now I give half of my possessions to the poor, and if I have cheated anybody out of anything, I will pay back four times the amount.'

Jesus said to him, 'Today salvation has come to this house, because this man, too, is a son of Abraham. For the Son of Man came to seek and to save what was lost.' (Luke 19:1–10)

Jericho was a very wealthy and important town. It lay in the Jordan valley and served as a major customs site for goods entering Palestine from the East, and this made Jericho one of the greatest taxation centres in Palestine. Now of course Palestine was still a country subject to the Romans, and tax collectors were employed by the Romans and were therefore regarded as traitors.

Taxation was very complex. For example, there was a poll tax that all men from the ages of fourteen to sixty-five and all woman from twelve to sixty-five had to pay just for existing. Then there was a ground tax that consisted of one-tenth of all grain grown, and one-fifth of wine and oil produced. Income tax was also payable, at 1 per cent of a man's income. On top of all this, there were all kinds of duties. A tax was payable for using the main roads, the harbours and the markets. A tax was payable on each cart – on each wheel, and on the animal that drew it. There was a purchase tax on certain articles, and there were import and export duties. I could go on and on. And you thought our current taxes were unfair!

Zacchaeus was a man who had reached the very top of his profession – he was the chief tax collector – and was the most hated man in the district. He was a social and religious outcast because he co-operated with the Roman government. There are three parts to his story from which we can learn some final lessons for sharing our faith.

He was wealthy but he wasn't happy

It's no surprise that Zacchaeus was rich because as we've seen he worked right in the middle of an important trade route. But he was unpopular and wouldn't have had much of a social life. Deep down he was desperately lonely, but had heard of this man, Jesus, who welcomed tax collectors and sinners, and wondered if he would have any words for him. Despised by everyone around him, Zacchaeus was reaching for the love of God.

There's a story that's told that comes from the sinking of the *Titanic*. A very wealthy woman eventually found her place in a lifeboat that was about to be lowered into the raging North Atlantic. She suddenly thought of something she needed, so she asked permission to return to her stateroom before they cast off. She was granted three minutes or they would have to leave without her. She ran across the deck that was already slanted at a dangerous angle. She raced through the casino with all the money that had rolled to one side, ankle deep. She came to her stateroom and quickly pushed aside her diamond rings and expensive bracelets and necklaces as she reached to the shelf above her bed and grabbed three small oranges. She quickly found her way back to the lifeboat and got in.

Now that seems incredible because thirty minutes earlier she would not have chosen a crate of oranges over even the smallest diamond. But death had boarded the *Titanic* and had transformed all values. Instantaneously, priceless things had become worthless. Worthless things had become priceless. And in that moment she preferred three small oranges to a crate of diamonds.

Many of your friends will be reaching for the love of God. They may have tasted wealth and prosperity as Zacchaeus did, and found them wanting. I once read about an encounter Alfred Lord Tennyson had with Queen Victoria in Buckingham Palace. The great poet commented, *'Up there, in all her glory and splendour, she was lonely.'* Your friends might not be royalty, but they may well have achieved success in other ways, yet deep down know there has to be more to life, and crave a purpose and a destiny. Let's help them reach out and find the love of God.

He wanted to see Jesus

For Zacchaeus to mingle with the crowd was a risky thing to do. He was a small man, but being so unpopular, no one would make room for him in the crowd. Instead, they'd probably take the chance to push, kick and nudge the little tax collector. Indeed he probably ended up black and blue with bruises that day. But he was so determined to see Jesus he wouldn't let anything stop him, so he ran on ahead and climbed a tree.

Billy Connolly, the Scottish comedian and actor, said this: *'I can't believe in Christianity, but I think Jesus was a wonderful man.'* I still meet people who think Jesus was some kind of first-century religious hippie who went around in a flowing white dress with a ring doughnut hovering above his head! The real Jesus was an incredible man, whose words were simple, yet profound. People were never the same after listening to him. Through our thoughts, words and deeds, let's show the world the real Jesus, a man who came to give life.

He showed everyone how he had changed

Zacchaeus was determined to show the entire community that he was a changed man. After his encounter with Jesus, Zacchaeus took a decision. He decided to give half of his goods to the poor, and to use the other half to make restitution for all the fraud he had committed. In this '*fourfold*' restitution he went far and beyond the Old Testament laws of restitution (Leviticus 6:1–5; Numbers 5:5–7). He showed by his actions that he was a changed man.

It's worth repeating again that when St Francis of Assisi had finished preparing his disciples for their work of evangelising the world, he gave one more instruction. When motivating and inspiring them to communicate the gospel, he reminded them that it would not simply be the words that they spoke which would reveal the heart of their message: '*If you have to, use words.*' St Francis knew that the most powerful sign would be for his disciples' lives and actions to communicate their message.

I've talked a lot in this book about communication techniques and ways to answer questions. These are important, but most of all let your life shine for Jesus and others will be attracted to the light. The story of Zacchaeus ends with the great words: '*For the Son of Man came to seek and to save what was lost.*' I've used the word 'lost' time and time again in this book, because it's a word that Jesus also used a lot. In the New Testament, 'lost' doesn't mean damned, unbeliever or non-Christian or anything like that. It means 'in the wrong place'. My keys are lost when they're not in my pocket and I don't know where they are. When I eventually find them, I put them back where they should be.

A person is lost when they have wandered away from God. Those you desire to know Jesus are also temporarily lost. There is hope for them – don't ever stop believing that. So let's agree to go forward and help them back to where they should be, in relationship with God.

Finally, remember the words of Paul – a man who persecuted

Christians until his encounter with God turned him into probably the greatest missionary of all time:

> Devote yourselves to prayer, being watchful and thankful. And pray for us, too, that God may open a door for our message, so that we may proclaim the mystery of Christ, for which I am in chains. Pray that I may proclaim it clearly, as I should. Be wise in the way you act towards outsiders; make the most of every opportunity. Let your conversation be always full of grace, seasoned with salt, so that you may know how to answer everyone. (Colossians 4: 2–6)

Stand united, singular in vision, contending for people's trust in the Message, the good news, not flinching or dodging in the slightest before the opposition. Your courage and unity will show them what they're up against: defeat for them, victory for you — and both because of God.

Paul the Apostle
Martyred in Rome, AD 65
(Philippians 1:27–8, *The Message*)

Appendix 1: Community Survey

Interviewer: Date:

Male/Female   Under 20   20–30   30–40   40–50   60+

1. How long have you lived in this neighbourhood?

2. How many people do you talk to on an average day?

3. What sort of neighbourhood is this?

4. Has it changed much over the years?

5. What do you see as the main problems in this area?

6. What could be changed to make it better?

7. What facilities are lacking in your neighbourhood?

8. Who would you turn to in a time of crisis?

9. Do you attend a church?

10. What would you like to see the Church do in this area?

Thank you for your time. Would you like to be informed of special events that [Arun Community] Church is putting on in the future?

Appendix 2: Beliefs Questionnaire

Interviewer: Date:

Male/Female   Under 20   20–30   30–40   40–50   60+

1. Do you have any religious   ....
   background?

2. Do you belong to a church?   *Yes / No*

3. How often do you attend   *Frequently / Seldom / Never*
   church?

4. Which of the following best describes you?

   Definitely believe in God   *Sometimes believe in God*

   Think you believe in God,   *Definitely do not believe in*
   but are not sure   *God*

5. When you die, what do you believe will happen to you?

   Will be reincarnated   *Will go to hell*
   Will cease to exist   *Don't know*
   Will go to heaven – eternal life   *Other* ....

6. Do you have a satisfying   *Yes / No*
   purpose in life?

7. What do you most want ....
   out of life?

8. Who do you think Jesus was?

   The Son of God　　　　　*A wicked con-man*
   A good moral teacher　　*Don't know*
   A mythical person　　　 *Other* ....

9. Why do you think Jesus died?

   Because he broke the law　*Don't know*
   Deliberately, for our sin　 *Other* ....

10. Do you believe Jesus rose again from the dead?

    Yes / No / Don't know

11. Do you believe God is interested in you personally?

    Yes / No / Don't know

12. If you could know God personally, as a friend, would you be interested?

    Yes / No / Don't know

Thank you for your time. Would you like to be informed of special events that [Arun Community] Church is putting on in the future?

Bibliography

Anderson, Sir N., *Evidence for the Resurrection* (IVP, 1950)

Anderson, Sir N., *Christianity and World Religions* (IVP, 1984)

Andrews, E. H., *God, Science and Evolution* (Evangelical Press, 1980)

Archer, G., *Encyclopedia of Bible Difficulties* (Zondervan, 1990)

Barton, A., *Questions of Science* (Kingsway, 1999)

Berry, R. J. (ed.), *Real Science, Real Faith* (Monarch, 1991)

Bruce, F. F., *The Books and the Parchments* (Fleming H. Revell Co., 1950; revised and updated 1984)

Bruce, F. F., *The New Testament Documents: Are They Reliable?* (IVP, 1960)

Burrell, M. C. and Wright, J. S., *Some Modern Faiths* (IVP, 1983)

Castle, F., *No Flowers ... Just Lots of Joy* (Kingsway, 1996)

Chapman, C., *The Case for Christianity* (Lion, 1981)

Christianity: A World Faith (Lion, 1985)

Cotterell, P., *This is Christianity* (Paternoster, 1997)

D. C. Talk and The Voice of the Martyrs, *Jesus Freaks* (Albury Publishing, 1999)

Field, D. and Toon, P., *Real Questions* (Lion, 1982)

Graham, B., *Just As I Am* (Harper Collins/Zondervan, 1997)

Grieve, V., *Your Verdict* (IVP, 1988)

Gumbel, N., *Searching Issues* (Kingsway, 1994)

Holder, R. D., *Nothing but Atoms and Molecules?* (Monarch, 1993)

John, J., *Calling Out* (Word Publishing, 2000)

Legg, S., *Man, Myth or Maybe More?* (Silver Fish, 1999)

Legg, S., *Big Questions* (Breakout Publishing, 2000)

Lewis, C. S., *Mere Christianity* (Fount, 1952)

Lewis, C. S., *Miracles* (Fontana, 1947)

Lewis, C. S., *The Problem of Pain* (Fount, 1940)

Lucas, E., *Genesis Today* (Christian Impact)

Lucas, J., *Lucas on Life* (Word, 2001)

McDowell, J., *More than a Carpenter* (Kingsway, 1979)

McDowell, J., *Evidence that Demands a Verdict* (Campus Crusade, 1972)

McDowell, J., *More Evidence that Demands a Verdict* (Campus Crusade)

McGrath, A., *Suffering* (Hodder & Stoughton, 1994)

Miller, B., *John Wesley* (Bethany House Publishers, 1973)

Morison, F., *Who Moved the Stone?* (Faber, 1930)

Polkinghorne, J., *Quarks, Chaos and Christianity* (SPCK, 1994)

Poole, M. W., *God and the Big Bang* (CPO, Worthing)

Poole, M. W., *A Guide to Science and Belief* (Lion, 1995)

Robinson, J., *Can We Trust the New Testament?* (Mowbrays)

Sayers, D. L, *Creed or Chaos* (Harcourt Brace, New York, 1999)

Stott, J. R. W., *Basic Christianity* (IVP, 1958)

Stott, J. R. W., *The Cross of Christ* (IVP, 1986)

Watson, D. C. K., *In Search of God* (Falcon)

Watson, D. C. K., *My God is Real* (Falcon, 1978)

Wilkinson, D. A., *God, the Big Bang and Stephen Hawking* (Monarch, 1996)

Wilson, R. D., *A Scientific Investigation of the Old Testament* (Moody Press)

Yonggi Cho, P., *Prayer, Key to Revival* (Word, 1983)

Young, J., *The Case against Christ* (Hodder & Stoughton, 1986)

Breakout!

The Breakout Trust is a registered charity, committed to communicating the relevance of the Christian faith. Its Director is Steve Legg, a Christian speaker, entertainer and writer.

Through humour and fun, Steve attempts to smash the misconceptions that many have about Christianity, and to show how faith in Jesus is not only reasonable, but very relevant and vitally important.

This he does in Britain and overseas in schools, colleges, universities, prisons and out on the streets. Face to face, and through the medium of radio and television, he has reached millions across the world, and seen thousands come to know the reality of the Christian faith for themselves.

Steve can be contacted at:

The Breakout Trust
PO Box 3070
Littlehampton BN17 6WX

Tel: 01903 732 190
E-mail: steve@breakout.org.uk
or visit the web site: www.breakout.org.uk